Princess RECOVERY

Princess RECOVERY

A How-To Guide to Raising
Strong, Empowered Girls
Who Can Create Their Own
Happily Ever Afters

Jennifer L. Hartstein, PsyD

Psychologist and CBS's *The Early Show* Contributor

Aadamsmedia

AVON, MASSACHUSETTS

Published by
Adams Media, a division of F+W Media, Inc.
57 Littlefield Street, Avon, MA 02322. U.S.A.
www.adamsmedia.com

ISBN 10: 1-4405-2795-4
ISBN 13: 978-1-4405-2795-1
eISBN 10: 1-4405-3183-8
eISBN 13: 978-1-4405-3183-5

Printed in the United States of America.

10 9 8 7 6 5 4 3 2 1

Library of Congress Cataloging-in-Publication Data
is available from the publisher.

This publication is designed to provide accurate and authoritative information
with regard to the subject matter covered. It is sold with the understanding
that the publisher is not engaged in rendering legal, accounting, or other
professional advice. If legal advice or other expert assistance is required, the
services of a competent professional person should be sought.
— From a *Declaration of Principles* jointly adopted by a Committee of the
American Bar Association and a Committee of Publishers and Associations

Many of the designations used by manufacturers and sellers to distinguish
their product are claimed as trademarks. Where those designations appear in
this book and Adams Media was aware of a trademark claim, the designations
have been printed with initial capital letters.

Crown on chapter openers istock 03-15-11 © nathan winter

This book is available at quantity discounts for bulk purchases.
For information, please call 1-800-289-0963.

Dedication

To all the heroines out there . . . enjoy wearing your crown as you play in the mud.

Acknowledgments

The idea for this book was presented to me by my editor Victoria Sandbrook, who believed I could bring a great deal of insight to it. Despite some worry, I jumped at the opportunity to help parents raise strong, feisty girls and enjoyed every minute of my time working on it. I so appreciate the opportunity to have written it.

I could not have done this without the help of Jennifer Lawler, who guided me through the process and was an excellent teacher along the way.

There are lots of amazing women out there working on passing along this message to parents and their girls. I could not have wrapped my brain around this topic without their blogs, websites, and information. Be sure to check out: Melissa Wardy's Pigtail Pals—Redefine Girly; Dr. Jennifer Shewmaker's Operation Transformation; and Hardy Girls Healthy Women, started by Lyn Mikel-Brown and Sharon Lamb. Their insights have been invaluable.

The incredible Lisa Marber-Rich has fought for me, backed me, and gotten me greater opportunities than I ever would have imagined. Who would have thought my little deal would have turned into this?

A special thanks goes out to my clients, who were patient and understanding of the time I needed to work on this book. You all enrich my lives in ways I could not possibly express, and I thank you for letting me be a part of your journey.

To Barbara and Joe, Alix, David, Sydney and Aaron: thank you for understanding that sometimes I just could not be around due to this commitment and for supporting me through it.

To Greg, Karen, and Sydney: your unwavering support and encouragement has gotten me through some of the times I just wanted to stop. And, a special thanks to Sydney for being the ultimate heroine.

My parents, Laura and Mike, have been the best examples of the lessons outlined in this book. They drove me from ballet to soccer as I changed in the back seat, and always encouraged me to chase the dreams I had, never putting limitations on anything I wanted to try. I would not be the woman I am today without their guidance and love. Thank you for all you have done, and continue to do for me.

To my husband, Mat. Thank you for believing that I could do this. Thank you for pushing me even when I pushed back. And, thank you for understanding when I had to stay up late working rather than hang out with you, then rubbing my back when I was so exhausted. I could not have done this without you. LUMM.

And, finally, to Hudson, whose wiggles and waggles made me smile every day.

Contents

INTRODUCTION
What Is Princess Syndrome?

Though you won't find it in any medical textbook, millions of young girls are living with Princess Syndrome every day. A girl with Princess Syndrome is focused on the fairy-tale of life: playing only with the pretty toys and dresses, regarding herself as the center of the universe; obsessed with how she looks, even if she's only headed to the playground. Full-blown Princess Syndrome forces a girl to be too dependent on others, to spend all her allowance on cosmetics and clothes, to care only about the things money can buy, and to think only of herself.

Sometimes, princess play is just that—harmless play. After all, gorgeous castles, elaborate gowns, sparkly jewelry, romantic rescues, and happily-ever-afters have been favorite playtime topics of girls for generations! But when taken to an extreme— and without positive messages to counteract it—princess play sucks little girls into a world where their self-worth is tied to their outward appearance, their happiness is based on the arrival of a prince who will love them, and their intelligence is something to be hidden rather than celebrated. And at a time when the media's influence is stronger than ever, girls are more repeatedly exposed to these rampant yet unhealthy messages than they were generations ago.

Parents do their best to help their daughters avoid this unfortunate malady. In today's contemporary society, with its obsession on appearance, the freshest celebrity gossip, and the hottest toys, their positive messages often get drowned out. Our daughters can't always hear us above all the other noise.

When young girls are first interested in princess play, parents often don't see how their daughters could possibly be affected by the underlying messages they are receiving. Well-meaning parents may believe, "My daughter is too smart to think those fairytales are the same as real life! She knows she doesn't need to be a size 2 to be beautiful! She knows she can build her own career instead of waiting for a rich man to marry! She knows she should help a girl in her class who's being bullied!" Yet, it takes more than smarts to resist social pressures and to undo the effects of ubiquitous advertising. Even if your daughter has heard you remind her of "the right things" a thousand times, would she have the high level of self-confidence necessary to implement them in her everyday life? She has an *inordinate* amount of pressure on her from a multitude of angles asking her to do just the opposite. Your influence has to outdo those pressures.

Some alarming studies have shown you do need to take action if you want your daughter to grow into a functional adult with good self-esteem, positive body image, and healthy moral values that will guide her through the difficulties of adulthood. For example, one recent study from the National Institute on Media and the Family showed that at age thirteen, 53 percent of American girls are "unhappy with their bodies." By the time they reach age seventeen, the number grows to a startling 78 percent.

According to *Medical News Today*, a December 2010 study showed the number of eating disorders in children under the age of twelve has risen 119 percent over the past few years, and children as young as four are being treated in hospitals and outpatient treatment centers for these issues. Just as alarming, researchers at Pepperdine University found girls as young as three are anxious about their body weight.

And that's just one aspect of Princess Syndrome: impaired body image combined with too much emphasis on outward appearances.

Beyond body image, girls run into problems because they are defining themselves by their friends' expectations. Young women leave adolescence feeling entitled to have a lot of pretty things—without putting in the work. As a result of not knowing themselves and focusing mostly on the external world, they engage in romantic and sexual relationships where physical and verbal abuse are the norm.

Without an intervention, the preschooler who insists she wear her Sunday best on the playground could easily become the party girl who can't hold down a normal relationship—much less a job. Does that sound like a dramatic jump? Sadly, it's not.

If you're a parent with a daughter who may have Princess Syndrome, it's important to know how to counteract these unfortunate messages. What can you do to make sure your daughter becomes the strong, independent woman you would like her to be? How can you help her build a healthy self-worth while allowing her to enjoy her favorite pastime—playing with princesses? It can seem overwhelming. You may not know where to start. That's where *Princess Recovery* comes in.

While you may feel the best course of action is to shield your daughter from these negative influences, you can't just take away her favorite toys, books, and movies and lock her in the highest room, in the tallest tower. Instead, you can show her how to deal with society's pressure and how to develop positive self-esteem, a realistic body image, and self-sufficiency.

In *Princess Recovery*, you'll learn how to replace the unhealthy "princess symptoms" with positive "heroine values" no matter what age your daughter is now.

THE PRINCESS . . .

- Prioritizes outer beauty before inner beauty
- Looks to others for help—instead of helping herself
- Feels entitled to the better half (or better whole) of everything
- Does things for the appearance of perfection
- Believes romance will fix a relationship
- Believes she'll eventually find and marry "The One"
- Defines herself by the way other people perceive her and her life
- Expects only the best for herself—and, depending on the type of princess she is, the best or worst for everyone else

THE HEROINE . . .

- Appreciates inner and outer beauty
- Helps herself—and others
- Works hard to earn her successes
- Does things for the right reasons—whether she's working to better her own life or someone else's
- Maintains healthy relationships with everyone she loves
- Believes in a bright future she's imagined for herself
- Defines herself confidently, by her own standards and moral compass
- Sets high yet attainable expectations for herself and balances her expectations of others with empathy and compassion

No child is perfect. Yours will likely struggle with some of these heroine values once in a while. Still, you want to offer your daughter a range of healthy and productive goals she can work toward. Will she stumble? Or course. Your job is to help her stay on track by showing how much you love her and by reinforcing positive messages.

HOW TO USE THIS BOOK

This book is a comprehensive program to help you prevent your daughter from falling prey to the unhealthy messages that princess play can impart. While you can read it cover-to-cover, you can also turn to specific chapters that address the problems about which you are most concerned.

Each chapter includes an explanation of a specific "princess symptom" and how parents, peers, and other social pressures may contribute to it, plus how it can be detrimental to your child in the long run. The behavior is clearly described, with examples of how it may show itself in your daughter's life. This is the core of each chapter's "Princess Symptom" section.

Each chapter also includes a healthy "value" that can counteract those symptoms. You'll find realistic ways to implement that value based on your child's age, with the emphasis on encouraging the wanted behavior rather than discouraging the unwanted behavior. Three age categories are used: ages 2–3, 4–5, and 6–8. You may find some suggestions for categories outside your daughter's age may also work depending on her personality and the presence of older siblings; these are loose guidelines, not set-in-stone rules.

You may fear the worst if you recognize any symptoms of Princess Syndrome in your daughter. But as you wade through the mountains of tulle, high-heeled shoes, and tiaras in your home, remember your little girl is most influenced by your love and positive messages. Embrace all the wonderful aspects of your daughter that make her who she is—even the princess-loving ones. Show her how to create her own "happily ever after"!

CHAPTER 1

The Problematic Lessons Your Daughter Learns

It seems harmless at first: a sweet story about a princess finding her prince and living happily ever after. Most of us want to marry and have families and be happy; what's wrong with that dream? If your daughter identifies with the princess, and wants to wear the princess shoes, and buy the princess dress, and own the princess doll, is that really so bad?

Well, you wouldn't be reading this book if you weren't worried and didn't think you already knew the answer.

None of these things are bad in and of themselves—the princess story isn't the problem, nor is your daughter imagining life as a princess. Pink shoes and sparkly dresses and feather boas aren't the problem. They become a problem—and the damage begins—because of the messages they send to your daughter, especially when those messages aren't counteracted elsewhere.

For example, that princess story may be teaching your daughter everything from "only appearances matter" to "don't expect to rely on yourself—you'll need a prince to rescue you." If this were just one story in a life full of all kinds of stories, it's no big deal—especially if you talk with her about how princess stories are different from real life. Unfortunately, your daughter's life may not be full of all kinds of stories. In fact, a lot of the stories your daughter is hearing send exactly the same messages.

The rest of this chapter outlines some of the messages your daughter, even at a very young age, is hearing from the media, from the culture around her, and from friends and family. Some of these lessons are intentional—when they appear in advertisements, for example. Others are unintentional—such as when a well-meaning family member repeatedly compliments her appearance—but can still be harmful. They are damaging to her because they create a false belief system about the world, and disempower her from taking control over her own life and becoming her own person.

PROBLEMATIC LESSON #1: GIRLS AND BOYS ARE VERY DIFFERENT

Over and over, children hear that boys and girls are different, not just in their physical appearances, but in their brains, hearts, and souls. They are told constantly girls like a certain type of toy while boys like another kind. Girls are given gifts of dolls and tea party sets; boys are given trucks and dinosaurs. Girls need to be rescued; boys do the rescuing. Some parents go so far as to jokingly roll their eyes at their rough-and-tumble sons while praising their quiet and docile daughters. This is just as true now as it ever was. While your child was born with some aspects of her personality and interests ingrained, others are introduced and reinforced by the world around her. The truth is that the development of gender identity is both innate and environmental.

For example, think of the stereotype that young boys like to run around and have a difficult time sitting still. Are girls innately any different? No. They enjoy exercise and fresh air as much as boys. Yet some "misbehaviors" that are typically accepted in boys (not being able to sit still at circle time, for example) are not tolerated in girls. Some teachers would criticize a girl for not being able to sit still, rather than laugh it off as just "how she is." That's how young girls get this unhealthy message—you're different than boys; sit still, be pretty and you'll succeed, be liked, and get more.

Reading Advertisements

To see how much environment and media reinforces stereotypes about girls and boys, even in the twenty-first century, pick up a circular from the Sunday paper, and turn to the toy section of a major retailer.

1. Look at the dolls being marketed to girls. What types are there? You probably won't see more than baby dolls and Barbie-like dolls. Dolls that look like young girls, such as the American Girl collection, aren't often found at a regular retailer.
2. Count the number of girls playing with sports equipment or being shown playing sports. Count the boys. Compare.
3. For sports equipment such as bikes, how can you tell it's being sold to girls? Hint: What color is the equipment?
4. Look at the toys marketed to boys. What types of toys are considered boys' toys? Now do the same for the girls' toys. What gender assumptions are made?

PROBLEMATIC LESSON #2: YOU SHOULD BE PRETTY

The idea that attractive people are "good" people has a long history. Think of Cinderella: Her mean stepsisters and her wicked stepmother are ugly, while Cinderella is beautiful. While what's considered beautiful may change over time, all societies and cultures have ideals they hold girls and women to. While expecting all girls and women to adhere to a specific beauty standard is at minimum highly unrealistic, the problem is made worse by social assumptions that beautiful people are by definition good people.

You would think we know better by now, right? After all, we're not the superstitious peasants of the eleventh century, equating the rare with the desirable and the outer with the inner.

A new educational program designed to stop bullying is called "Play Pretty, Play Pals." The part of the program aimed at girls is—you guessed it—the one called "Play Pretty." (The part for boys is called "Play Pals.") Even without expending much effort, it's easy to see the messages here:

1. Girls and boys play differently.
2. Girls should play pretty, which means nice. *Pretty* equals *nice*. Being a *pretty* girl equals being a *good* girl.

You can see how the underlying approach of this well-meaning program impacts how girls view themselves in the world.

If this were an isolated example, it wouldn't hold much weight. But it isn't an isolated example; it is an accepted cultural belief—so much so that, as studies have shown, you can make more money at a job just by being pretty. That's right: If you're pretty, you will make more money than someone else with the same skills who isn't pretty, or isn't pretty in the dominant culture's accepted view.

PROBLEMATIC LESSON #3: THE MORE YOU HAVE, THE BETTER YOU ARE

You only have to watch television for ten minutes to realize marketers don't sell goods and services, they sell dreams and fantasies. If you buy this beer, you'll get dates with attractive women (interesting, strong, determined, and world-changing women need not apply). If you buy this car, you'll live in a mansion like this, with a beautiful wife like that, and not have a care in the world.

Children are sold similar dreams, only their messages arrive in louder and more colorful forms. If you buy this toy, you'll have lots of friends. If you wear this dress, you'll be a princess, and everyone will adore you.

Our society makes judgments all the time about where people fit in the world based on what they own. If you work in a job where it's important to your success to dress nicely or own an expensive car, then you know how this plays out in the real world. It's just as true for your daughter as it is for you. If she wears jeans from Target while everyone else is decked out in clothing from The Gap, her status definitely drops. Depending on the environment (not all schools or peer groups are the same), this is not simply her perception, but it can be an actual fact of her life.

Unfortunately, as parents, we often encourage conformity instead of individuality. We see what is happening and, not wanting our daughter to feel left out, we buy the Gap jeans, thus reinforcing the message that fitting in and wearing what everyone else does is the best (and safest) option.

PROBLEMATIC LESSON #4: SOMEONE ELSE WILL RESCUE YOU

Snow White is rescued by the prince who kisses her, Sleeping Beauty by the prince who kisses her, Jasmine by the street rat pretending to be a prince (he outsmarts the bad guy; no kissing necessary). Television and movies are full of women-in-jeopardy plots, in which said women are rarely, if ever, the instruments of their own deliverance. Not only do these tales reinforce the idea that, when in trouble, someone else will come to the rescue (especially if you are pretty!), this message prevents young girls from learning how to problem-solve and to rely on themselves.

But all of that is fantasy, right? We hope our girls can tell the difference. Unfortunately, it's not so easy, and, as a parent, you may unintentionally reinforce the idea that she can always be rescued by someone else. For example, if your daughter forgets her homework for the millionth time, do you run home, pick it up, and drop it off at school on your lunch hour? (You wouldn't want her to get in trouble with a teacher!) If a peer is being unkind, rather than work with your daughter to find solutions for the situation, do you immediately call the parent of the other child involved and demand that something be done?

It may feel like you are just doing your job as her parent, but rushing in to protect your daughter from being hurt or disappointed creates a fragility in her. Such fragility makes it difficult for her to grow strong enough to take care of herself. It also reinforces the belief she needs help from others to do anything. It teaches her she can't rely on herself, or figure out how to fix her own mistakes. Of course, you need to love and support your daughter in a way that's appropriate for her age. But ask yourself if you're simultaneously teaching her how to do that on her own when the time is right.

If your daughter learns to be reliant on external things and people, she may have a difficult time building self-reliance, which interferes with her finding her own worth. "I can do it myself!" is not just the battle-cry of a toddler; it is a necessary component of self-esteem. Although your intention is good when you try to solve your daughter's problems for her, the outcome can be damaging to her sense of self, as she never learns to pick herself up when she falls.

PROBLEMATIC LESSON #5: YOU SHOULD BE SEXY

Probably the most damaging message your daughter is hearing (and she hears it over and over) is that her only value is in her body—that her brains, her talents, her kindnesses are unimportant. The only reason anyone would be attracted to her is because of her body, especially the size of her breasts and the length of her legs. This sexualization of young girls is an ever-present, ever-worsening problem that can cripple your daughter's ability to grow into a healthy young woman with a strong sense of selfhood.

Here's just one example. In early 2011, clothing retailer Abercrombie & Fitch introduced a line of padded swimsuits for young girls (age seven to fourteen). The bikinis included bra tops that were originally called the "Ashley pushup triangle." For the low, low price of $24.50, parents could ensure their eight-year-olds looked as sexy as possible at the swimming pool.

After the ensuing furor died down, Abercrombie & Fitch recategorized the swimsuits (giving them another name) but continued selling them. Clearly, Abercrombie & Fitch thought there was a market for such swimsuits. Why? Because people buy them.

Most parents do not think, "I want my daughter to be considered a sexual object at the age of eight!" Instead, they think "it's cute," or they suppose it doesn't matter when their daughter asks for one ("all the other kids have them!"), or they just don't stop to consider the messages they're sending—and the messages they're confirming: *You're only worthwhile if you're attractive. Your body isn't good enough without a little help from your clothing.*

Of course, you can refuse to buy these items, but that doesn't always solve the problem. After all, relatives or friends could buy them as a gift. Or, your child could buy them with her own money—it is more and more common for tweens to go shopping alone with their friends, and they aren't always going to use good judgment in their purchases. Tweens are as susceptible to marketing as the next person, if not more so. They are influenced not only by advertisements, but by the way products are displayed, with the promise you can be just a little more grown-up when you buy this swimsuit or this pair of shoes or these panties with the funny saying.

Yet an eight-year-old girl isn't consciously thinking, "I am ready to express my sexuality!" She's thinking, "I'd look pretty in that!" "My friends all have it, now I will, too!" or "I'll look like my big sister/idol/favorite actress." This is an important distinction because it shows that a child of that age isn't ready for that kind of clothing.

The Marketing of Sexy

Whether she's ready for it or not, your young daughter is being targeted in ads for sexy clothes. The relentless marketing of sexy has a long history. For many years, the subject—and object—of such marketing was adults. Grown people have, one assumes, already formed a sense of themselves and their self-worth and know how to effectively interpret the messages they are being bombarded with. With each passing year, however, marketing seems to focus on a younger and younger demographic, until you have two-year-olds worried about their body image, and mothers putting their toddlers on unnecessary diets.

Of course, we can't solely place the blame on marketing. Nor can we solely blame parents who don't say no to inappropriate clothing. There is a host of problems to consider which include peer pressure and the wider culture in which our children live.

The APA's (American Psychological Association) Task Force on the Sexualization of Girls found that sexualization occurs when any of the following happen:

- A girl's value is perceived to be only in her sexual attractiveness. Nothing else matters.
- Physical attractiveness is equated with sexiness—that is, as being available as a sexual object.

- A girl is made into a sexual object—a thing—rather than a person with thoughts and feelings of her own, the ability to make decisions and to take actions.
- Sexuality is imposed on a girl too young to understand the consequences; the sexuality being imposed isn't a normal girl's exploration of physical and emotional feelings related to sexuality but is inappropriate and does not come from within.

Numerous studies have shown that women, especially young women, are depicted in the media primarily as sexual objects and must conform to a very specific standard of beauty. This is what your daughter constantly sees and so it is no surprise if she copies it, even if she doesn't understand it.

Yet it isn't only the media that promotes this sexualization of girls. Parents do it, too, especially when they believe—and send the message—that an attractive appearance is more important than other goals for girls. For example, a parent who buys the padded swimsuit, or who encourages dieting for looks as opposed to healthy eating, is sending the message that how a girl's body looks matters more than other considerations. It happens when a parent chooses to enroll her daughter in beauty pageants rather than dance classes or soccer leagues and when she is praised more for how pretty she looks than how well she is doing in school.

Premature sexualization can be reinforced by peers, as girls pressure each other to conform to societal standards of attractiveness and sexiness. It gets perpetuated even further when boys harass girls about their appearance because boys, too, are impacted by the messages they see on television and elsewhere. They may tease a flat-chested girl—even if she is in a completely normal developmental stage! Eventually, of course, girls internalize these behaviors and begin to evaluate themselves solely based on how they look.

Sexualization of girls isn't trivial or unimportant. It has devastating and long-lasting effects on girls, as the APA reports:

The Effects of Early Sexualization

- When a girl starts to think of herself as an object, which happens when others sexualize her, she is less likely to do well in school because it affects her ability to focus; the same thing doesn't happen to boys.
- Emotionally, such objectification makes a girl feel less confident with herself and less comfortable with her body.
- Objectification makes a girl feel shame, anger, and disgust.
- Mental health problems such as eating disorders, low self-esteem, and depression are related to sexualization, as is substance abuse.
- Physical consequences may result from the mental health disorders related to sexualization.
- Sexualization does not create healthy sexuality; it leads to diminished sexual health, including early promiscuity.
- Sexualization reinforces stereotypes about girls and women. Girls who have more exposure to early sexualization are more rigid in their beliefs about women's roles.
- When boys and men are exposed to girls' sexualization, they find it harder to connect with real girls and women (with all their flaws and imperfections) and have difficulty maintaining intimate relationships—which becomes a problem for heterosexual girls and women.
- Sexualization results in sexism in society, resulting in fewer opportunities for girls and women.

How Early Sexualization Plays Out

The truly unfortunate part—often minimized by parents and society—is what the image of a sexy eight-year-old presents. An eight-year-old boy isn't going to care if his eight-year-old counterpart is in that Abercrombie & Fitch padded bathing suit. He just wants to swim and have fun. The problem is, a young girl looking older than her age may attract the attention of an older boy, or a man. It may seem flattering and fun at first, but young girls don't know how to interpret the behavior nor how to navigate unwanted sexual attention. Learning to be sexy too young has been found to put young girls at risk for negative relationships and early sexual acting-out as they develop into young women, according to the APA Task Force on the Sexualization of Girls.

The bottom line is if a girl learns she'll get lots of attention for being coy and pretty—and yes, even sexy—she'll use that as she grows to get what she wants, rather than using her intelligence or athleticism, for example. Teach your daughter the importance of respecting herself and her body, as this will decrease the risk of abuse and sexual acting-out and help her build a sense of empowerment. We'll discuss more about this topic in Chapter 9.

Make Sure You're the Role Model You Need to Be

A few years ago, Playboy Bunny and actress Shauna Sand reportedly released a sex tape when her three daughters were at an impressionable age. It doesn't take a parenting expert to realize this was probably not the best idea ever. And who can forget Alec Baldwin trashing his daughter in a voicemail, saying, in part, "You don't have the brains or the decency as a human being. . . . You are a rude, thoughtless little pig"? While you may comfort yourself that you don't have this kind of bad judgment, have you thought about what you *are* communicating to your daughter about her value—and about the value of women in general?

At the end of the day, it's up to parents to be the role model their girls need them to be. While all parents have their biases and unhealthy thought patterns, critically examining your attitudes can help you become a more positive role model. Taking these steps can help you be the person you want your daughter to emulate:

- Remember your daughter is watching you—and learning from you—all the time. Yes, that's a big responsibility, but it also means you have lots of opportunities to teach the right things.
- Let your daughter see your confidence in yourself. But don't think you have to be infallible or perfect. Admitting you make mistakes, making amends, and apologizing shows your daughter what it's like to be a real human.
- Respect others, including your daughter. If you find yourself making a lot of judgmental comments about others, make it a priority to stop. This is especially important if your comments have to do with superficial appearances.

MARKETING AND AGE COMPRESSION

You can see how these lessons can be detrimental to your young daughter. But how is it that marketers include such unhealthy, inaccurate, and adult messages and content in advertising campaigns, shows, and movies aimed at children?

Much of it stems from what marketers would consider marketing smarts: They understand children want to be like their older peers, so they devise messages that show how younger children can be like their older idols and role models. A younger sister wants to be like her older sister; her older sister wants to be like the college girl next door.

Before marketers get a hold of it, this natural tendency for a younger person to model herself after an older one is simply a way of exploring the next stage of development. Each subsequent stage of a child's life allows more freedom and autonomy, so the next stage is always more attractive to a child than the one she's in now. A two-year-old wants to be old enough to stop holding Mommy's hand; a five-year-old wants to be old enough to ride a bike; a thirteen-year-old wants to be old enough to drive a car.

Marketers understand this perfectly, which is why they market to teenagers in such a way that makes teenagers feel like adults, and to younger children in a way that makes them feel like teenagers. Such "age compression" means marketers are looking at what interests older children and then selling it to younger children; the younger children buy it (or want their parents to buy it) because they think it makes them like the older children. The age compression can continue until two-year-olds are being given vampire dolls based on a craze originally started by twenty-year-olds.

In other words, this is how we end up with bikinis with push-up bras marketed to eight-year-olds. It is also a symptom of a larger problem: our society's fixation on sex, sexuality, and attractiveness. While working to change society is a worthy cause, you need to begin at home to protect your daughter from this damage as much as you can.

While it may seem like there's a lot to battle, don't despair! Regardless of your daughter's age, you can run interference and begin to shift the focus from how she looks to what she can accomplish (or has accomplished). If you begin to address her efforts and to praise other parts of her (intelligence, for example), she will begin to recognize the positive things she brings to the table—things that will make her a heroine, not a princess.

CHAPTER 2

The Princess Recovery Program

Despite the widespread influence of media, society, and your daughter's peers, you're not helpless when it comes to protecting your daughter from the influences that can derail her. You can guide her along a path that will more likely help her develop a strong sense of values and a solid sense of self.

While tackling this problem is easier the earlier in your daughter's life you begin, you can make a difference no matter what her age. Even if you're afraid that your daughter is already a little princess, you can do something about it. You can teach her how to become a heroine.

THE BUILDING BLOCKS OF PRINCESS RECOVERY

The bad news, as you've heard: many forces are trying to influence your daughter. The good news? The Princess Recovery Program is mostly aimed at you, the parent, and what steps you should be taking in helping your daughter identify how marketers, society, and friends can pressure her in ways that are not in her best interest. *You* are the most important ingredient in the mix. And unlike what she hears from the rest of the world, you can control the messages you send! That means you need to be committed to making, and sticking with, the necessary changes to help your daughter become the amazing woman she is capable of being.

Here is the framework of the program:

Step #1: Recognize the Issues

The program begins with your ability to recognize these negative princess influences exist, and be aware of their prevalence and the exact messages they send.

Step #2: Create an Individual Plan

Next, you need to develop a personalized strategy for preventing your daughter from being overly impressed by these messages. Your strategy will vary, depending on your daughter's age and specific interests. Younger children can be shielded a bit more than older children can; your older daughter needs your guidance more than she needs your protection. Throughout this book, you'll find age-targeted recommendations to help you with this process. A recommendation made for a younger child may also work for an older one and vice versa (as long as you take into consideration your child's development and ability to understand). The main thing to remember is to have a game plan for dealing with these negative influences. That way, when Grandma shows up with five Barbies and a Dream House, you'll know what to do. Lack of preparation often results in giving in—and giving up—when it's not necessary. The core of the Princess Recovery Program is in developing this game plan—learning how to limit the influence of negative messages, thoughts, and behaviors, and learning how to encourage positive ones.

Step #3: Decide on Your Family's Values

Most important, you need to consider the values you want to instill in your daughter, and then model those values every day, with every decision you make. Yes, it can be exhausting to say no frequently (especially when that may mean saying no to yourself!), or to have to take the long view when the short one would be easier. Of course, you can expect to make mistakes along the way—but don't give up. Learning to make changes in your behavior will help you to combat Princess Syndrome— and raise your own heroine.

Throughout, we'll talk about how to replace each princess symptom with a heroine ideal, which will help your daughter embrace all positive aspects of herself, leading her to become a strong, empowered girl and later, a strong, empowered woman.

PROTECTING YOUR DAUGHTER WITHOUT LOCKING HER IN A TOWER

All parents have different influences they want to protect their daughters from (some people don't want fried foods, others don't want Barbies; the list is long). Sometimes it seems the best way to keep your daughter safe from the potential evils of the world around her is to just make her stay home with the television unplugged and only wholesome books and educational games available for her entertainment.

Someday, though, your daughter will leave home. In the unlikely event that such an overly protective approach would work, she would find herself an adult in a world she is ill-equipped to navigate or manage. That means you have to protect her while also teaching her what she may experience in the world and how to cope with it. It is your job to prepare her for what she'll encounter while helping her gain the smarts not to listen to most of it.

To put it simply, you're not wrong to think that protection can help, as long as you don't believe it's all you have to do, or that you can do it forever. In fact, one of the most important ways you can help your daughter when she is young is to shield her from damaging marketing messages. This means, to a large extent, protecting her from the media. Study after study shows it isn't one particular advertisement or show or song that causes the "princess problem," it is the accumulation of all the advertisements and shows and songs. It's entirely a numbers game: the more your daughter is exposed to, the more likely she is to buy into the stereotypes, no matter what you say or model to the contrary.

That doesn't mean you have to give away your television and donate all her princess toys. It does mean you should reduce and monitor her exposure to it. According to A. C. Nielsen statistics, children between the ages of two to five spend about twenty-two hours a week watching television (about one-quarter of the time they're awake), while older kids, up to age eighteen, spend more than four hours a day in front of televisions, plus additional time in front of computers. That's a lot of exposure to messages you may not agree with and your daughter probably doesn't need to hear.

What if you could turn those numbers around, though? What if you spent at least some of those hours each week engaged with your child? Really engaged—playing games (even princess ones!), singing songs, talking about your day (and hers), learning to do things together. Imagine the difference that would make. If it's a numbers game—the more times your daughter hears a certain message, the more likely she is to believe it—then you can make that work to your advantage by skewing the numbers in your favor. And the more people you have on board with your mission, the higher the likelihood the positive messages will come across.

PARENTING ON THE SAME PAGE

The first person who needs to get on board is your parenting partner. Good, bad, or otherwise, parents do not agree on all things. Sometimes, certain issues are just more important to one parent than to the other. Other times, as in the case of divorce, one parent has very limited say in what the other does. This certainly makes implementing the Princess Recovery Program more of a challenge. How can you work with your partner to figure out what's best for your daughter?

Get Your Partner's Buy-In First

Just as in all the other relationships in your life, you cannot make unilateral rules and expect everyone to follow. If your partner is not immediately on board, you may have to spend some time explaining to him or her specifically why you think this program is valuable.

> ## SMART SMALL
> You may feel the urge to push for more commitment or more involvement, especially if you feel your partner is not on board "enough." Compromise is the key here. Begin at a level both of you are comfortable with and build from there.

Begin by highlighting the perils of Princess Syndrome for your daughter, sticking to the facts and avoiding dramatic oversimplifications. You want to be serious and factual but not sound like you're going off the deep end because your three-year-old loves Cinderella. Discuss why you think making some of the changes outlined in this book will be good for your daughter's development and be open to having a discussion about it. Really listen to what your partner says about these ideas and concepts. Then ask what changes your partner feels he or she can stand behind and be committed to.

Continuously Build Your Partner's Awareness

You wouldn't be considering a program like this if you were not aware of the intensity of damaging messages your daughter sees, and worried that media and peer influences are greater than your influence as a parent. Your partner may just be awakening to the concerns that you have been aware of for a while.

Provide ongoing opportunities for education on this topic to your partner. Share different examples of advertisements, television programs, and general environmental influences with your partner, so he/she understands what is really going on outside of your home. You don't need to constantly belabor the point, but you can show your partner some of the more egregious examples of harmful messages you come across, as well as studies and other reports you see that explain the long-term harm they do. You may find once your partner really becomes awake to the issue, he or she may become even more vigilant about it than you!

Making Decisions with an Ex

There are many things in life you cannot control, despite your ongoing desire to do so. This is especially true if you are a divorced parent. Just because you and your ex decided your relationship didn't work doesn't mean you don't still have to work together. You have gone from partners to co-parents. As difficult as it is, you, as co-parents, need to figure out how to work together to raise the best children you can. You have to, despite the difficulty, put aside your differences and focus on how you want to raise your daughter.

Even with your best efforts, the rules in one house are not always the rules in the other house. Pick your battles. Decide what really matters to you and what you can let go. In the end, all you can focus on and control is what happens in your house, and what you (both parents) can agree upon. Hopefully, your styles are not so different so as to confuse your child, and, further, you will be able to come up with some compromises about how you want things to be in raising your daughter, especially as it relates to combating Princess Syndrome. If you feel your views are light-years apart, consider seeking the help of a professional family counselor.

Another key element is to keep your frustrations with your ex away from your children; do not criticize your ex in front of them. Although it may be tempting, it isn't going to help at all, and, in fact, can create worry and even depression within your daughter, which will interfere with her building up her sense of self. If your child asks why the rules are different at your house, you can simply say, "Your daddy (or mommy) and I have different ways of doing things. The rules may not be the same at both of our houses, and that may be confusing for you. But we both love you very much and are doing the best we can to create the best home for you in both our houses. If you're ever confused, just ask us what the right choice is." The more you can present a united front, even when separated, the better off your children will be.

GENERAL TECHNIQUES FOR REINFORCING POSITIVE MESSAGES

Your daughter is going to be exposed to media messages, marketing, peer influences, and societal expectations no matter how careful you are to protect her in your own home. Instead of trying to keep her free from all potentially negative influences, you can take steps that will help you manage those influences and give her a context for what she's hearing and seeing. Most of all, make sure you constantly affirm and reinforce the values you want her to have. You will see variations on these techniques in many of the chapters of this book. They are the core methods you'll use to teach her.

Talk about What She Sees and Reads

When your daughter watches television or movies, do your best to watch with her whenever possible. Instead of banning the *Beauty and the Beast* DVD, turn it into a learning experience. Point out how Belle uses coy and indirect language instead of firmly and directly saying, "Leave me alone" to Gaston. Ask your daughter how things may have been different had Belle clearly communicated what she wanted (and didn't want). Then have the same fun with the Beast. Discuss why he may act as he does, why he has difficulty trusting, and how things may have been different for him had he not had the life he had—if he had made different choices.

If that conversation is too sophisticated for your young daughter, instead talk about your thoughts regarding what *you* see in the movie. Do you think it's important for your daughter to believe that love has a transformative power? If so, you can focus on that message. ("Love teaches the Beast he can be a better person. Because he loves Belle, he makes the effort to change—and he does change.") That way, *you* can decide what the movie is about. If you think it's important for your daughter to maintain strong family ties, talk about how Belle and her father support and love each other; each makes sacrifices for the other. You can even talk about how Gaston uses his language and behavior to convince the villagers to do bad and thoughtless things! He can be an example of bullying behavior and how dangerous it can be.

Beyond television and movies, another area to focus on is what your daughter reads, including the websites she visits. Read the same books, magazines, and online sites your daughter reads. Talk about the headlines. Ask her specifically why she wants certain products. If she's old enough, ask what she thinks the ads are trying to get her to buy into, and see if she believes them.

Discuss Choices

Many times during your daughter's development, she will want things you won't want to buy or don't think are good choices. Even though you may say no to what she wants, it's important to understand why she wants and likes the things she does. This helps you understand her better and can help you guide her to making more appropriate choices.

For example, if your daughter wants to buy a shirt you think is inappropriate, ask what she likes about it instead of dismissing the purchase outright. You may be surprised by her answer. You may assume one thing, when in fact she likes it for entirely different reasons—maybe she likes the color or the length or the sleeves, and isn't aware it would show her bellybutton or it has an inappropriate message written on the front. (Even if she can read the words, she may not understand the inappropriateness of the message.)

It's so important to show that you understand why she wants to make the choices she does (her friends have it, she has seen it on television, it's "cool") and guide her toward making choices more likely to affirm her self-image and build her confidence.

Say No

If you don't want your child to watch certain shows, play with certain toys, or wear certain clothes, say no. As difficult as it may be, it's crucial to do. As best you can based on her age, explain why you are saying no, as that usually results in better understanding and acceptance. If your three-year-old wants the glittery princess dress, you can say, "That would be hard to play in! Let's try this sundress with shorts." If your nine-year-old asks to watch a PG-13 or R-rated movie, explain the language and situations in the movie are meant for older children and adults and suggest a more appropriate choice instead.

Just because your child may see the shows or play with the toys elsewhere doesn't mean your message won't be heard loud and clear if you choose not to have them in your own home. The more consistent you are in your message at home, the more likely your daughter will be able to follow—and live by—that message elsewhere.

Encourage Other Outlets

Help your daughter find areas of interest that don't focus on her looks or attractiveness, but that rely on skill and abilities she can learn and enjoy her whole life. Sports, music, volunteering—there are many outlets for your daughter's energy that don't put the focus on her physical appearance.

Discuss what your daughter may be interested in. While she is very young, you get to choose all of the different activities in which she participates. As she grows, she will develop preferences. Have ongoing dialogues about what she likes and dislikes and build on those interests. The more confidence she gains through learning new skills, the less focused she will be on how she looks doing it.

Talk Often

To help your daughter focus on what matters most, an important first step is to *listen*. Listen to what she thinks, what she wants, what is meaningful to her, how she feels about things, and why she feels that way. Although we often think this conversation doesn't have to happen until girls are pre-teens and teenagers, it can start in toddlerhood. Take every moment possible to talk with your daughter. Obviously, as her language skills improve, so will the chats. The earlier you promote open conversation, the more likely it is you'll be having these conversations on into the teen years, when they are equally as important. Listen nonjudgmentally and with as open a mind as possible.

Eventually, you'll get to the point where you can begin having conversations with serious topics. For example, start early discussing what appropriate sexuality is, even if the conversation is uncomfortable. During this conversation, be sure to talk about making good choices and speak about what makes a healthy relationship. We'll talk more about this in Chapter 10.

Further, lead by example when *you* talk. Remember that she is listening to what you say, even when you're not having a direct conversation with her. Don't judge others by their appearance, and remind your daughter not to focus on this as well. As humans, we often focus on either the beautiful or the "weird." Broaden this out and encourage your daughter to see the whole person, not just the parts. If you begin to do this as well, she will follow your lead.

Complain to the Management

Although it may feel as though you have few choices or no power in changing the messages bombarding your daughter, that couldn't be further from the truth. When companies and organizations promote sexualization, stereotyping, or other inappropriate representations of young girls and women, speak out. Find ways to get your concerns heard. If your daughter is old enough, have her help you with this step: look up the name of the manufacturer or producer, find contact information, write and send the complaint to the company, explaining why you think what they are doing is inappropriate. It's amazing what this can do to help effect change, even when you don't think it can. You can also discuss why not to buy the products and work with your daughter to find products that promote positive messages.

SKILLS TO TEACH YOUR DAUGHTER

As you build your own awareness of how the media and society influence Princess Syndrome, you must simultaneously help your daughter increase *her* awareness. In age-appropriate ways, you can do the following:

Ask Questions about the Media

Teach your daughter to ask questions about the media she consumes. Model this when she's young so that as she gets older she can ask questions such as:

- "Why is that doll something I want?"
- "Why is that piece of clothing so skimpy?"
- "Why do I like that celebrity—for how she looks or for what she does?"
- "Why do people care what I look like?"
- "What do I admire about people other than how they look?"
- "What do I like about myself?"
- "Is what other people think of me important to me?"

These questions help your daughter be a discerning consumer as well as an empowered girl.

Dress Appropriately

Help her learn to dress in appropriate ways. Focus on the practicalities more than the message she is sending, especially with young children. You probably don't want to get into a discussion with your five-year-old about why five-year-olds shouldn't look sexy. Point out how choosing something "easier" to wear may be a better option: "You have to keep adjusting that shirt. Maybe it would be better to wear something that doesn't distract you so much." You don't want to thwart your girl's individuality, yet you do want to promote a healthy sense of appearance.

Speak Up

Encourage your daughter to speak up, not only to ask questions but to discuss when something uncomfortable happens, either to her or someone else. If she comes to you with a question or concern, take it seriously and give it careful attention. This will reinforce her behavior as you affirm the idea that speaking up does get you help.

All too often our girls stay quiet for fear of getting into trouble, letting someone down, or being a tattletale. If you start listening and communicating early, your daughter will realize you are her ally and you want to help her live in a safe, supportive space. If she feels that from you, she will continue to use your connection throughout her development.

Conformity Isn't Required

While helping your daughter learn to choose appropriate toys, games, and clothes, you will sometimes discover she wants something because her peers have it. One way to deal with this is to guide her in understanding that conformity is not all it is cracked up to be. Help her realize that just because someone else has something doesn't mean she has to have it, too. Individuality is good! Encourage her to make her own choices and to embrace her differences. This is an important step on her journey to selfhood. Although it may be "easier" to be the same as the crowd, if your daughter is not true to herself, she'll end up making bad choices that could create more emotional difficulties. Learning to be comfortable in her own skin will protect her from making negative choices. Teaching this often and early can be a great protective factor.

HELPING VERY YOUNG CHILDREN

As noted, these conversations must be tailored to the needs of your child. You wouldn't dress your two-year-old and your twelve-year-old in the same outfits. Similarly, you wouldn't have the same conversation with both. Although the underlying message may be the same, the delivery has to be different.

Preschools and Daycare

Though you can largely control what you allow in your own house, you don't have the same control regarding exposure at other people's houses, in daycare, or at preschool. Studies show that about 70 percent of preschools allow television viewing, and they may be showing things you wouldn't at home. In addition to the media saturation in these settings, you are likely to find other things you don't approve of and wouldn't have in your own home.

Here's the hard truth: It is inescapable that your daughter will encounter a Barbie along the way. In fact, if you walk into most daycare settings or schools, even the most enlightened and gender-neutral, chances are, you *will* stumble across a Barbie (or another toy or message to which you object). That doesn't mean you must immediately find a new place to take your daughter. It may mean you have to have a conversation with the educational staff about promoting the use of skill-building toys, or it may mean that you donate more suitable toys. And keep in mind that your daughter may surprise you. She may have no interest in Barbie and may prefer other activities more. If you start encouraging healthy play early, and if you expose your daughter to those kinds of toys and activities in your own home, it will carry over into other parts of her life.

Perhaps what is most important is a caregiver's attitude toward children, especially girls. This is likely to have more of an impact than whether he or she allows the children to watch too many princess movies or has more dolls than educational toys in the toy box. If the caregiver (which includes you, grandparents, teachers, nannies, and so on), thinks in stereotypes, your daughter will have much more to overcome. Unfortunately, some of the behavior is automatic and is done without thought. If you want your children, both boys and girls, to get the most well-rounded experience, you need to be aware of these attitudes and recognize how they affect your children.

You're Still #1

You, her parent, are her first teacher, and will, at day's end, have the greatest influence on her life. Rather than focusing too much on the Barbie at daycare, sit on the floor with your daughter when you get home and play a game—even if only for a few minutes before you get pulled in another direction. The more you emphasize the ways that things can be negative ("Barbies are bad"), or push your disapproval on your daughter ("You should never play with Barbies!"), the more enticing the forbidden object becomes and she'll end up playing with Barbie every chance she gets. If you keep the focus on the positive, empowering activities, ignoring rather than bashing the toys you dislike, you'll have a greater chance of promoting positive choices. As with anything, if it seems too taboo, it increases the interest. Since you probably won't get rid of Barbie, encourage healthy Barbie play instead. Talk about what kind of job Barbie might have. Ask her what Barbie's favorite toy might be. Find out who Barbie's friends are and what they like to do. Even a two- or three-year-old can engage in pretend play at that level—a level beyond what Barbie's wearing and when Ken is coming home. Focus on the things that promote the attitude you want to foster, and you'll be surprised how your daughter starts to internalize the positives instead of the negatives.

DEALING WITH GIFTS

Situations where your daughter receives gifts can pose a unique challenge. After all, not everyone has your awareness, or shares your concerns, or even has the same goals and values that you have. In fact, there may be people, including your family and close friends, who think you are creating problems where there don't need to be any. Your awareness will inevitably lead to a situation when what you want rubs up against what someone else does. For example, suppose it's your daughter's fifth birthday, and someone brings her a Bratz doll or another toy you don't like and/or don't want her to have. How do you handle that? What will you say or do? Once again, it is your job as her parent to be the gatekeeper. That may mean accepting a toy but not allowing it to be used. It may mean returning the gift. And it may mean talking to the giver about why this isn't the kind of gift/activity you want your daughter around. As hard as it is to have conversations about these things, it is very important to discuss your expectations with the important people in your daughter's life.

Educate Gently

As a parent, you need to speak up, but you need to do it in such a way that you will be heard and respected. If your neighbor gives your daughter an inappropriate toy, your initial reaction may be: "You may not care that everyone in the neighborhood calls your daughter Lolita behind your back, but frankly, I don't want that for my daughter," but expressing that sentiment out loud is not the best idea. It's certainly not going to get your point of view heard, and, in fact, may create more conflict. Insulting people won't change their minds; it just makes them angry with you.

Your best bet is to speak your mind by stating your case clearly and with appreciation: "Thank you for the gift. I know your daughter has fun with those dolls, but we prefer to have our daughter play with dolls that are more age-appropriate. Although we appreciate it, this isn't the kind of doll we'd like her to have. If you'd like to keep it for your own daughter, please do!"

Be Specific

As you educate those around you, make sure they really understand. When you say you like gender-neutral toys,

Grandma may not know what you mean. In fact, she may think you mean "not girly" and bring over a toy cap gun and some ammunition, which may not have been exactly the result you were after. Explain what you mean and why you are making the request. Have a dialogue about why this is important to you and to the development of your daughter's healthy self. Then, make your requests *very* specific. For example, you can say, "She's interested in collecting rocks, so check out your garden for any cool rocks she might like. And she always loves art supplies, especially markers and stickers." Providing guidance can only increase understanding, decrease conflicts, and promote positive interactions.

Consider the Relationship . . .

No matter how much you hate the doll from the Monster High collection your sister-in-law gave your daughter, remember it's just a hunk of plastic that, when all is said and done, can get "lost" or accidentally fall into the "toys to donate" bin. If making a fuss over the gift is going to irreparably harm your relationship with the giver, and your relationship with the giver matters to you, be gracious, accept the gift, even if you don't like it, and remind yourself that it is only one item in a world full of options. By talking about the gift with your daughter, and by promoting healthy play with it, or offering completely different alternatives of toys you approve of, any negative message is dulled down and the experience is less damaging.

. . . But Advocate for Your Daughter

You also need to advocate for you daughter and teach her to advocate for herself. Talk to your daughter about why you think the gift is inappropriate in a way she can understand, by using language related to her age. Be prepared for lots of questions, possibly some tantrums, and don't make promises that you can't keep. Here are some suggestions for how to have the you-can't-have-it conversation:

- Say something like: "This is a toy for older children. We'll put it away and you can have it later." Say this only if it's true and that you'd let her have it when she's older. She may forget about it, but what if she doesn't? Some kids have amazing memories.
- "Your dad and I don't approve of violent toys. Here's why."
- "This isn't a toy we think will teach you positive things. Let's go look for other options." The key is to identify your values, why the toy doesn't match them, and then communicate that decision to your daughter in a way she can understand.

Then, do whatever you must to follow through on your decision: return it to the store, donate it, give it to the dog. Help your daughter decide on a toy that is more appropriate: "A doll that looks more like you would be more fun!"

YOUR RULES IN OTHER PEOPLE'S HOUSES

You're the parent at your house, so your rules go. If that means no vampire dolls are invited across the threshold, then that's what it means. Enforcing the rules can be tricky, and your daughter may not always like it, but since you're in charge, it's not a completely impossible task.

When your daughter visits places outside your home, your authority and control are obviously more limited. Grandma's house may be heaven for your daughter, but all you can see is the television blaring at all hours of the day and night. The next-door neighbor may be really nice, and her kids are always polite, but they appear to have erected a shrine to Disney princesses in their basement. Your daughter's best friend from school has a mom who thinks letting a six-year-old wear the word "juicy" emblazoned across her butt is funny.

What do you do? How do you navigate the waters for and with your daughter when you can't even get on the boat? This is a big dilemma, and, as a parent, it is your job to create the structure that gives your daughter the best chance to grow up to become a healthy adult. To this end, you need to offer ideas and be supportive of your daughter when she encounters messages and behaviors you disagree with. This is challenging, especially in those situations where you are not present to monitor exactly what's going on. Here are some suggestions that may help.

Just Say No

It is okay to stick to your values and set limits on what your daughter is able to do. If your daughter is invited to participate in something you feel is inappropriate, and you know you will not be comfortable if she goes, then you have to say no, and you have to have an open and honest conversation with your daughter about why, using age-appropriate language. A meltdown will surely follow, but stay strong in your convictions that at this point in her life, you know what's best for her.

As hard as it may be, you may also have to have a direct conversation with the host about why you are choosing to keep your daughter from participating. You could say something like, "Thank you for the invitation, but we don't let our daughter watch PG-13 movies."

For another example, there's a trend where a group of young girls all go to the spa for a manicure and pedicure party. How do you deal with an invitation like this? Assess your own feelings about it. You may feel it is totally harmless and just in good fun. Or, you may feel it is sending the wrong message to girls, that looking pretty is the best way to have fun.

If you decide to let your daughter go, talk to her about it beforehand, saying something like, "The most important part of this day is that we're spending time with some good friends. Getting our nails done is fun, but I'm really looking forward to hearing how Madison's trip to Florida went and how Emma's soccer team did in their tournament. What about you?"

Whatever your choice is, identify your values and stick to them.

Make Your Expectations Clear

As a consumer, you have the right to ask for certain things. If you take your daughter to daycare, or if you have a nanny, you can make it clear you expect your daughter to be engaged in some sort of meaningful activity for a significant part of the day instead of having her parked in front of princess movies or playing with older girls' dolls for eight hours a day. If this expectation is not met, you have the option of taking your business elsewhere, or firing the person working for you.

Although it may be more difficult, you can have the same expectations with your family and friends. It is harder to draw the line with them, of course, and not only because you can't just fire them. For example, well-meaning Grandma and Grandpa may think it is their prerogative to spoil your daughter and create a little princess. You can (and should) have an open conversation about what you would like them to do when they do spend time with your child. Your parents may think what worked for you will also work for your daughter, and they may not be as aware of all of the images and messages your child is being bombarded with. In fact, you may have to educate them about why and how things are different, so they understand and can support your position. Just remember to respect their position, too—they're likely very excited to have a granddaughter and want the best for her too. Together, find ways that they can enjoy spending time with her while also enforcing the values you want to instill in her.

Turnabout Is Fair Play

It's absolutely fair to ask for what you want, but reciprocation is equally fair. Your neighbors, siblings, and friends will have preferences and rules for their children, the same as you do, and it goes without saying that these rules must be respected, even if you don't agree. You cannot expect your preferences to be followed if you minimize those of your friends and family. You may think a hot dog is perfectly harmless and a healthy lunch, but for the family down the street that practices veganism, feeding one to their child despite their request you not do so, is just as offensive as their giving your daughter that Fashion Barbie play set.

You do not live in isolation. Your children will play with other children, and your families will intermingle, so it is important to have these conversations with your friends and the parents of your daughter's friends, so you know what their expectations are of you, and you of them.

Look on the Bright Side

Every challenging decision you face can be a teachable moment for you and your daughter. Take the idea of a "spa day" party. On the surface, it may seem like a bad idea for a young girl. There is something to be said for not encouraging obsessiveness with appearance. But, in fact, getting a manicure and a pedicure is often a fun thing women do together, so why not little girls? In fact, there are so many other wonderful elements of the party to consider: socialization with her friends, learning patience while she waits her turn, making decisions about a nail polish color. You may be surprised at what aspects of the party stand out to your daughter: giggling with her friends, being excited for the birthday girl when she opens her gifts, eating cake. The nail polish may be totally a nonissue.

If you encourage your daughter to focus on the elements of the party that are not appearance-based, such as spending time with friends, laughing, and having fun, that will be what your daughter remembers. Shift the focus to the non-appearance-based things, and your daughter will start to appreciate the positive relationship-building elements of the day, not the appearance-enhancing ones.

It's vital for girls to learn the importance of strong, healthy relationships, especially with female peers. If those experiences can be highlighted and strengthened when girls are young, it will help them develop these kinds of relationships as adults.

STARTING OUT

The Princess Recovery Program aims to provide you with tools to help you raise a strong, intelligent, well-rounded daughter. She will be pulled in many directions to act in certain ways, think in certain ways, and behave in certain ways. You, as her parent, must use your influence to help direct what these ways may be. The most important thing to remember as you begin is that communication—with your daughter and those who love her—is crucial. If most of the important people in your daughter's life know and can reinforce your position, your efforts will go even farther. At the very least, if you provide enough of a foundation in your own home, what goes on outside of it will have less impact.

Now that you have identified for yourself what Princess Syndrome is, and how it can impact your daughter's development, it's time to figure out what to do about it. Chapter 3 will help you get started.

CHAPTER 3

Value Brains over Beauty

PRINCESS SYMPTOM: Appearances Are Everything
HEROINE VALUE: Smarts Pay Off

HOW BAD IS IT OUT THERE?

Everywhere your daughter looks are images showing women with airbrushed, Photoshopped beauty, unattainable in the real world—or only attainable in the most unhealthy of ways. Here are some simple facts that help illustrate this point:

- The average model is 23 percent thinner than the average woman, according to a study done by the Just Think Foundation, a media literacy organization.
- Thirty-five percent of occasional dieters develop pathological dieting issues, according to the National Eating Disorders Association.
- Young girls are more afraid of being fat than of losing their parents—or of nuclear war, says a study on body image conducted by the University of Colorado-Boulder.
- According to the Girls, Women + Media Project, teens report that TV, movies, and other media are some of their leading sources for information about sex and sexuality.

Beyond those facts, a report by the American Academy of Pediatrics (AAP) reveals that on average, a young TV viewer will see about 14,000 references to sex each year, with only a small fraction including any reference to abstinence or delaying sex, using birth control, pregnancy risk, or sexually transmitted disease.

This AAP study also found that with this early repeated exposure comes a greater risk of teens engaging in sexual relations earlier. To take it a step further, the studies show the younger a girl is when she has sex, the more likely she is to have engaged in it due to pressure from her partner, or even due to force.

Gender differences also are present. More often than not, in advertising, music videos, and video games, men are fully clothed, while women are often in the background exposing some part of their bodies, or wearing tight, revealing clothing.

These types of statistics may not be news to you. What you may *not* know, however, is how great the impact of these messages can be on a girl's sense of self. In fact, one of the more damaging effects of Princess Syndrome is a poor body image. The impact of a poor body image is wide-reaching and can influence a girl's mental health, leading to a great deal of unhappiness and anxiety even if it does not rise to the level of a diagnosed disorder.

THE PRINCESS SYMPTOM: APPEARANCES ARE EVERYTHING

This message invades your daughter's daily routine. As her parent, your message comes through the loudest. If you're constantly on a diet, frequently berating yourself for eating too much, or sighing every time you look in the mirror, you're communicating your dislike for your body and making your daughter wonder if she should be just as worried about hers as well.

The idea that "appearance is everything" is more than just what your body looks like, however. It also includes a preoccupation with things that will enhance your appearance, such as clothing, cosmetics, and hairstyles. This obsession with appearance can also extend to comparisons with others, celebrities and noncelebrities alike. You'll read more about these issues in Chapter 6. For now, let's look at how these types of worries regarding body can negatively impact your daughter's life.

What Is Body Image?

Body image is how you feel about your own physical appearance. Virtually everyone has an opinion about this subject, even if it isn't something they're obsessed about. Body image is what you "see" when you look in the mirror, or when you think about your physical appearance. Most of us, especially women, think about our physical appearance a lot.

When your thoughts about your body become distorted, you imagine you look a way that is inaccurate. People with distorted body images see themselves in ways that are simply not true. For example, if you have a distorted body image, you may be at a physically healthy weight—not too thin and not too fat, but right where you need to be for your height and build—but still see yourself as obese and unattractive. This could lead you to diet and exercise in unhealthy ways, and will have a negative impact on your self-esteem, and may create anxiety and depression.

Body image is heavily influenced by what you *believe* about what you see. Your thoughts have a direct impact on your feelings and behaviors. If you believe something, even if there is evidence to the contrary, it triggers all sorts of emotions and reactions within you. For example, if you observe you've gained some weight, what are your thoughts about it? Is your initial thought a calm, problem-solving idea, such as: "I notice I've put on a few pounds, and that doesn't make me feel so healthy. Maybe I should cut back on desserts or alcohol for a while and increase my exercise." Or, do you immediately jump to negative, judgmental thoughts, such as: "I am so gross and disgusting! Who would ever love a fat cow like me? I'm never going to leave the house again!" Even if you don't say those thoughts aloud, your daughter can recognize which position you take.

Body image and your thoughts and judgment about yourself are not only impacted by how you think about yourself, but also by how you believe other people view you. This is especially true for women, and, unfortunately, the worry over other people's perceptions begins at a very young age.

Despite what you may have heard, women are the biggest culprits of objectifying themselves and others, often trying to achieve unrealistic standards based on observations of actresses, models, and the like. Women (and girls) are affected by how they think they're being seen, especially as they are aware their appearance affects how others perceive them — and, sometimes how they are *valued* by others. The external pressure becomes internalized, and can result in many problematic behaviors such as disordered eating, compulsive shopping, self-injury, depression, and anxiety.

It is important to understand the difference between dealing with a constant negative body image versus generally having a positive body image, with a few negative thoughts once in a while. We all have days when we don't feel great in our skin, when we just don't feel like we look the way we want, or we simply don't feel good in a particular outfit that we have chosen. This is a typical experience that happens on occasion to everyone.

What Is Negative Body Image?

A negative body image means your ideas about yourself are uncomfortable almost all day, every day. You don't really see what is there and judgments and negative ideas run the show when it comes to your views of your body. It's almost as if you can't see the reality. You believe you're not attractive, even with information to the contrary. You believe your body is "wrong," "bad," and so on. These thoughts lead to feelings of shame about yourself and your body, and have the result of making you feel uncomfortable and awkward in your environment. It can be a never-ending cycle where the discomfort and awkwardness feed into your negative body image.

What Is Positive Body Image?

On the flip side, having a positive body image is seeing what your body truly looks like, flaws and all, *and understanding that your appearance does not communicate your worth as a person.* You have healthy ideas about your body and take care of yourself so you can maintain these feelings. You eat right and exercise (most of the time!) in order to be healthy, not because you are focused on being the thinnest or fittest. With a positive body image, you are not consumed with thoughts about your looks. You feel confident and comfortable in your own skin, which sets the stage for more positive things all around.

Consequences of Poor Body Image

There are serious, even devastating, consequences associated with struggling with a poor body image. People with poor body images are more likely to have disordered eating habits. While you may be aware this includes anorexia or bulimia, you may not realize it also includes obesity. Overeating, or compulsively eating too much, can be just as much a reaction to societal pressures as dieting too much. The physical consequences of disordered eating are many, and the psychological risks are great. Those with severe anorexia and bulimia may have hair loss, loss of muscle and bone mass, liver and kidney problems, even heart attacks. Individuals fighting obesity face an increased risk for type 2 diabetes, heart attack, and stroke.

The problems with a severely impaired body image are not purely physical. Poor body image can also lead to psychological and emotional problems, and can include:

- Anxiety
- Depression
- Low self-esteem
- Engaging in nonsuicidal self-injurious behaviors
- Suicidal thinking
- Shame
- Difficulty concentrating
- Isolation
- Risk-taking with health, especially sexual health

Harmful Attitudes Toward Less-Than-Perfect Bodies

It's clear that we have to take a step back and look at how to manage our critical judgments. This is especially important when the ideals presented to us are so often unattainable. A March 30, 2011 *New York Times* article explored how Western prejudices against people who are overweight have spread around the world. While the article itself was an interesting analysis of how media influences perceptions, it was the comments from readers that provided the most insight into how our culture really views overweight people. Within the public comment section after the article, readers expressed such enormous hatred and vitriol toward people who are overweight it's no wonder our children are overly focused on how they look.

Trying to find some compassion, even self-compassion, in the hundreds of comments on the piece is very difficult. For example:

- "I've never met a successful person who was overweight."
- "If my partner were to get fat, that would be grounds for breakup."
- "Fat people are lazy, gluttonous, unattractive, and self-centered."

It's amazing to see what people really think about overweight people in a society where a significant percentage of the population is considered overweight. What does that say about how these people might feel about themselves? And how is this message getting translated to our children, especially young girls?

Generally, people tend to think being overweight is entirely volitional and under a person's control. A "fat" person is choosing to be fat and just isn't trying enough. Overweight people are thought of as lazy, ugly, unsuccessful, self-loathing, and stupid. Never is any sort of cultural influence, physical problem, or the like considered to be part of the issue. These snap judgments occur even before the observer has had a chance to learn anything about the overweight individual, who may, in fact, be successful, industrious, and happy. Unfortunately, appearance is often the first impression made on another individual, and if you don't fit the "mold," you can be rejected before you ever get a chance to participate.

Many studies have shown how the exposure to media can influence poor body image and disordered eating, which is exactly what this *Times* article concluded—wherever mass media spreads, poor body image and eating disorders follow, even in cultures that previously didn't have narrow definitions of beauty.

SELF-CARE FOR MOMS AND DADS

All of this information highlights the importance of protecting your daughter from too much media, so you can prevent her from buying into the grossly unrealistic fantasies about what women should look like. Whenever you can, point out strong, healthy girls and women in the media and how they are confident and determined. These are some incredibly important things that you can start doing for your daughter now.

The other most important thing you can, and must, do? Work toward acceptance of your own body. Here are some ways to do that:

(Try to) Love What You See in the Mirror

You may be struggling with your own body image — many of us are. If stepping on the scale has the capacity to ruin your day, your daughter will notice that. It's extremely important not to communicate your dislike of your own body to your daughter. As you know, you are the role model she looks up to, and she will follow your lead. If you can begin to accept yourself, flaws and all, she will begin to accept hers as well. In fact, maybe it's time to accept and appreciate your body just as it is. Rather than concentrating on how you don't look like the twenty-year-old you used to be — your body is not as tight, there are wrinkles around your eyes — note the strong arms you have from carrying your kids around and the toned thighs you've sculpted from squatting to get the laundry out of the dryer a million times. You have been trained for a long time to be judgmental of yourself. Start to let go of those judgments and embrace who you are.

Take a Healthy Approach to Food

Hand in hand with embracing your body is taking a positive, proactive approach to eating well. Begin by turning around your negative self-talk. Instead of saying, "I ate too much! I'm such a pig!" remember your daughter is listening and watching. Instead, try something like, "My tummy is telling me that I ate too many cookies! I'm going to go for a walk to help digest. Want to come?"

Offer Nutritious Options

Work with your daughter on making healthy food choices. If you don't keep unhealthy, sugary foods in the house, they won't become her (or your!) "go-to" choices for a snack. Model what it means to be healthy, not only in the way you speak to yourself, but in your actions. You probably won't eat perfectly balanced meals every day—but perfection is not what you're trying to instill as a goal. Acknowledge slip-ups and make efforts to remedy them by eating better the next day. Build in activities that will keep you fit. Express when you feel good about yourself, and teach your daughter that this is okay to do!

Avoid the Clean Plate Club

As a society, we still have an unhealthy relationship with food. Fast-food restaurants are still plentiful, and although they are offering more healthy options, your children are not gravitating to them first, I'm sure. Additionally, some parents tell their children, "Eat everything on your plate!" They're not just talking about the vegetables, but also about the cheesy pasta and the French fries. This isn't the greatest idea, and it may be time to consider not taking this stance with your children.

Studies have shown children and adults eat in a healthier way if they regulate their own intake of food—that is, if they eat when they're hungry and stop when they're not. This gives them control (always an important issue for children) and teaches them to listen to their body's hunger signals. You may worry they're wasting food, but gaining unnecessary pounds isn't a good thing either! Instead, offer small portions and give seconds if they're still hungry. And there's no shame in bringing a doggie bag home from the restaurant.

You may worry your child won't get enough healthy food (i.e., fruits and veggies) by eating this way. The key is to offer nutritious options, and make sure it is more plentiful than the less healthy stuff. In fact, if you want your child to eat those vegetables, you may have to insist at least some portion of it is eaten before a "treat" can be had. As long as the good stuff is available, and outweighs the bad stuff by a considerable amount, your child will almost certainly do just fine. For more information about nutrition, talk to your daughter's pediatrician.

Think Aloud

A young child doesn't need to know the science behind calorie input and expenditure. She just needs to know healthy eating helps her body stay healthy. She also needs to know what healthy eating is—and she'll learn that from watching you. This is a case where modeling works better than monitoring. Instead of asking, "Do you *really* need another piece of toast?" which could make her feel ashamed of being hungry, simply talk about *your* decisions. "That pizza sure smells good! But I've already had one slice, and that's enough pizza for me!" Or, "I've already had one slice. I'm going to eat some of this salad to fill me the rest of the way up." If your daughter asks about why you will be eating salad instead of more pizza, explain your decisions to her.

You can model this with any food choice. "Those cupcakes look yummy! But I am trying to eat healthy food so I can stay healthy. I'm going to grab this apple instead. I think apples are delicious!" As you model, however, remember your daughter should enjoy treats now and then, and she may not need to maintain as strict a diet as you. The key is balance and moderation for everyone!

Talk the Talk

Think about how you greet a girlfriend you haven't seen in some time. Generally after the hug and kiss hello, one of you will mention how great the other one looks. It's one of the first things we do. Though you both mean well in making the compliment, your daughter observes this and internalizes it as one of the primary ways of interacting with girlfriends: commenting on appearance first and foremost. Make conscious efforts to break this habit. Instead of commenting solely on how pretty a friend looks, focus on who she is and what she does. That will teach your daughter to focus on effort and good intentions. By focusing on the effort, your daughter cannot fail—she can always make an effort, whereas she *can* fail at looking pretty or being cute. That's not to say you should *never* tell her (or a friend of yours) that she looks pretty. You absolutely should praise your daughter if she looks particularly nice or worked hard to pick out a special outfit for a birthday party. But it is crucial to focus on other aspects of your daughter's life as well.

Promoting a sense of success will also help her to feel good about herself. Consider telling your daughter things such as:

- "It was very kind of you to help Jacob get his shoes on."
- "Wow! You sure can throw that ball hard!"
- "You do a great job of listening to the teacher at dance class."
- "I love how you used so much color in this drawing."
- "You should be really proud that you were able to finish your homework all by yourself. Great job!"

In replacing negative messages with more affirming ones, you're stressing the importance of intelligence and effort. Pretty can't solve the world's problems, or even what to make for dinner tonight, but intelligence can.

THE HEROINE VALUE: SMARTS PAY OFF

Although it may be difficult and require extra work, it's important to find other things your daughter can rely on outside of her appearance. If she finds activities she enjoys, she'll find them rewarding and you'll have plenty of opportunity to reinforce the value of hard work. If she loves to draw, enroll her in art class and encourage her to build on this strength. Perhaps she loves to read, and so do some of her friends. Create a book club for the girls. The more opportunities your daughter has to feel confident in other areas, the less the appearance will be her primary go-to for self-worth.

Adjust *Your* Attitude Toward Education

Take a minute to step back and consider any biases you may have toward being smart versus being pretty. Are you sending a mixed message to your daughter? You might be and not even realize it. Many people have an anti-intellectual bias and reveal reverse-snobbish attitudes. Maybe you've even said something like, "Ugh, Mrs. Smith has a lot of book sense but no common sense! I'd rather have common sense." The truth is, of course, you can be highly intelligent *and* have common sense. In fact, showing your daughter how to develop common sense as well as intelligence is certainly a step in the right direction. Focusing on the development of practical skills means you are giving her the solid foundation that will help her focus on matters other than appearance.

Appreciate All Kinds of Brain Power

Your little girl has many kinds of strengths, abilities, and talents, and it's important to notice them. Not every little girl is going to grow up to be president. Not every little girl is going to *want* to be president. Recognize that there are different kinds of intelligence—emotional, social, and intellectual. Just as a president has an admirable kind of intelligence, someone who shows good leadership skills also has an admirable kind of intelligence. It's the same with someone who is empathetic and compassionate. It is so important to stress these qualities when you talk about people, so you can educate your daughter on the different kinds of intelligences that exist. For example, you may say things like:

- "My boss is a really good leader. He doesn't always understand the computer programming I do, but he understands how to get me the help I need to do my job. I think that's really smart."
- "Your friend Sami is so kind. She really takes the time to listen when you have a problem and wants to help you when she can. What a great quality to have."

These statements can highlight to your daughter all the options she can explore.

Admire Intelligence

We are quick to provide positive feedback to people when they are attractive, saying "Wow, she looks great! She lost a lot of weight and is just so pretty now!" We are not as quick to say, "Wow, she is so smart! She did an amazing job on that project." Your daughter, being the sponge that she is, picks up on this discrepancy and learns she will get more attention and feedback the more attractive she is.

Start to praise people, especially women, for their intelligence and hard work in ways your daughter can understand:

- "Mrs. Kennedy sure knows a lot about math! She seems like a really good teacher. What do you think?"

- "Sally really did some good problem-solving about how to have a playdate today, despite everyone being so busy. Don't you think that was creative of her?"

If you can do this as often as possible, your daughter will begin to internalize the message that trying to be smart and having character is more important than how she looks.

DIG DEEPER

When these individuals come up in conversation, talk with your daughter about all aspects of the people she likes. She may love Lady Gaga, for example. Find out why. Maybe she does think she is a good songwriter, and doesn't focus on the outfits. If so, talk about some of her lyrics that promote self-empowerment and acceptance. And if she does focus on Lady Gaga's appearance, turn it into a discussion about individuality and creativity, two things you want to support in your daughter as well.

Tell Your Daughter about Intelligent Girls and Women

Find examples in the media of people who are both attractive and bright. Share these with your daughter to let her know you don't have to choose; you can have both. Talk about famous women and girls who have done remarkable things and have used their smarts rather than their beauty to achieve things — or maybe they have used both. Think Hillary Rodham Clinton versus Lady Gaga. Clinton is not known for her appearance, and yet she is one of the most powerful women in the United States. Through her education and commitment to learning, she was able to be a senator, run for president of the United States, and become the Secretary of State, meeting with world leaders and being involved in important global politics. Lady Gaga is an amazing force to be reckoned with, but unfortunately, sometimes her positive message and abundant talent gets lost because we focus on her appearance more than the other things. Her choice to push the envelope and wear crazy outfits means her smarts and accomplishments often get overlooked. There are many popular culture stars who fall into this trap. Their appearance becomes the topic of conversation, not their brains or their abilities.

Focus on the Whole Person

It can be tricky to find a balance between appreciating a healthy body and respecting hard work. You want her to value her brains, of course, and you want her to feel good in her own skin. Perhaps what is most important is that she sees herself as a whole person, not just parts. When you talk about her body, talk about how strong it is, how well she moves, how quickly she can run. Make sure she understands you value what *your* body can do. "I love being able to shovel the driveway without getting too tired" or even "I'll race you to the back fence!" The more integrated you are in discussing who and what she is, the more she will understand it, internalize it, and believe it.

AGE-APPROPRIATE SOLUTIONS FOR THE "APPEARANCES ARE EVERYTHING" SYMPTOM

Try these approaches with your daughter to help ensure she doesn't get too caught up in appearances. Remember sometimes children go through phases where they focus on things you wish they wouldn't focus on, but try to be patient and remain committed to your efforts. Even when you don't think the message is sinking in, it is, and you will be surprised by her understanding when it reveals itself.

Ages 2–3

Your daughter is still young enough that certain conversations may go right over her head. Have them anyway! She'll take in more than you know, and you'll get into practice for when she's older and the conversations become more in-depth.

Many people find toddlers adorable, and they may tell her that all the time. Often, they focus on appearances: "She's so cute! Look at her in that hat, what a gorgeous little girl!" There's nothing wrong with a little praise of appearance, but make sure that isn't the only thing your daughter is hearing. Say things like:

- "You did a great job helping Daddy clean your room!"
- "Look how strong you are! Those books you're carrying are very heavy."
- "Thank you for getting into your carseat without complaining. That's a great attitude."

When you read aloud to her, pick books that don't reinforce stereotypes about appearance. *The Paper Bag Princess* is a fun one that turns the typical princess story on its head.

Offer her some toys that don't reinforce stereotypes. During this age, you want to expose your daughter to everything possible. Encourage her to play with anything and everything presented to her and let her choose what she wants.

Give her variety in her wardrobe. If all you offer her is pink, and all you have are princess clothes for dress-up play, you are giving the message the only thing to be is a princess. Kids this age love to dress up: provide options. Let her dress up as a knight or a doctor or a firefighter.

Don't be afraid to say no. It may mean tolerating a tantrum, especially because at this age your daughter's tolerance for "no" isn't so great. If you really believe that princess costume isn't what you want for her, take a stand and say so. As the parent, this is your right, and you can share this opinion early, even if you meet with lots of resistance. If you don't want to go "cold turkey," here are some ways to make dress-up a more positive experience:

- Offer an alternative to princess dress-up: "I'd rather we dress up as something else, so I found these fun animal costumes. Do you want to be the lion or the rabbit?"
- Switch up the princess roles: "This time *I'm* going to be the princess. Do you want to be the prince or the evil stepmother?"
- Encourage creativity: "How about we make our own dress-up outfits instead? I'm tired of pink, so I'm going to pick out only things that are red! What about you?"

Ages 4–5

Your daughter might be starting to read a little bit on her own, so make sure she's supplied with good books that communicate the values you want her to have: that smarts are more important than appearance; that a person's value is in who they are, not what they look like. Your daughter, at this age, is also becoming more attuned to the "norm" and wanting to fit in with others. Try reading *Violet the Pilot*, about a bright girl who builds planes (and doesn't fit in because of that) and saves a troop of Boy Scouts.

Girls this age also love dress-up and pretend play. There's nothing wrong with the occasional pink boa, but girls can also dress up as pioneer women, judges, and in Mom's old business suit. If your daughter's pretend play continues to focus on living in castles, make a subtle change and talk about how she might *design and build* the castle. Draw out an estate and talk about what amenities it would have.

Encourage your daughter to get outside and run and play, jump and climb. There is no reason for her not to be as active as her male counterparts. Fight the message that she needs to be quiet and docile.

Ages 6–8

Older girls are more aware of peers and more susceptible to peer pressure. They are finding their place in a social structure at school and want to fit in. Wanting to fit in will be an ongoing theme, so make sure you have a solid strategy for dealing with it. Remind her while it's fun to fit in, friends don't have to be exactly alike. Be sure she knows it isn't worth changing who you are in hopes that someone will like you for it.

Talk about what makes a good friend. What qualities does she feel that she brings to the table and what qualities does she want her friends to have?

Have your daughter participate in lots of different activities (but don't overschedule her), so she can find what she really likes. Have conversations with your daughter about the vast possibilities of things available to her and help her decide what she may want to explore. It's okay for her to try a smattering of things—the point at this stage is to broaden her horizons, not to force her to continue an activity she doesn't like. Listen to her requests and try what she wants, not what you think she should want.

This is a great age to promote living healthfully. Work on creating meals together and finding time to do some family exercise.

Although these changes may seem overwhelming, they are doable. The earlier you start, the better. Start, as in all things, with yourself, and make the necessary changes in your own thinking. If you can start to think differently about what it is to be a girl, it will be easier to pass along these ideas to your daughter. When you start to implement these changes, you will, hopefully, begin to notice a shift from the princess mentality to that of a heroine.

CHAPTER 4

Banish Materialism

**PRINCESS SYMPTOM: What You Have,
Not What You Are
HEROINE VALUE: Pursue Your Passions**

THE PROBLEM WITH "THINGS"

We all have things, we all like things, and we all find things to
be useful in our lives. We often want to have more things, either
because we believe something more or different is better than
what we have, or we just *want* it, for no special reason.

It's not that material goods are bad in and of themselves. Try
to cook dinner without a stove, a skillet, and a spatula; you'll
be sending out for Chinese in no time. The problem is created
when we get bogged down in the things, using them to define
us, rather than having things that help enhance our lives in
some way, to make it easier, more comfortable, and more effective. When we're focused on what our things say about us, that's
when we're caught up in materialism.

Materialism is actually a very old philosophical argument
about the nature of the world, but for the purposes of this book,
we're going to use its popular meaning: "Only possessions matter, and the higher status they are (the more expensive, osten-
tatious, and luxurious), the better." It is interesting to note

materialism as a philosophy also says only physical objects matter, and the rest is ephemera.

Everywhere your daughter looks, she, too, is getting the message that what you possess is a measure of your worth as a person. Turn on an awards show and the commentary is as much about the clothes and jewelry the guests are wearing as about the accomplishments for which they are being lauded. At school, whoever brings in the newest smartphone or the coolest backpack gets all of the attention, and all the excitement, from the other students. In contrast, the child who earns a good grade on a test or spends the weekend planting a garden receives very little positive reinforcement from her peers. In fact, these actions seem so insignificant she could be dismissed or even criticized for her efforts.

In recent times, researchers have found downsides to getting wrapped up in materialism, both for adults and children. Although as a society we seem to believe you will be happier the more things you have, the reverse is actually found to be true. Focusing too much on the external can create problems in relationships, damage self-esteem, and increase feelings of depression and anxiety. Moreover, materialism prevents you from focusing on the things that really will help you increase your happiness—things like friendships, fulfilling work, and family. Materialism creates the same problems in adults and children, especially adolescents.

In a study in the *Journal of Consumer Research*, researchers found a causal relationship between materialism and self-esteem in teens—that is, self-esteem and materialism are connected in such a way that changes in one affect the other. Low self-esteem may increase an investment in materialism: meaning, if you feel badly about yourself, you're more likely to buy things to feel better about yourself. However, increasing self-esteem can cause a decrease in materialism: if you feel good about yourself, you don't need to surround yourself with things to feel better. The researchers found even small adjustments made to help improve self-esteem can have a profound effect on a child's or teen's materialistic viewpoint. Clearly, if you can create feelings of satisfaction and an improved, and positive, sense of self, the need to surround yourself with "stuff" to find self-worth will decrease. It does give you pause, doesn't it? What if you focused on improving your daughter's self-esteem (or your own) instead of buying things?

THE PRINCESS SYMPTOM: WHAT YOU HAVE, NOT WHAT YOU ARE

The culture of acquiring things is pervasive in our society. For example, how do parents often reward children? By giving them gifts! You've almost certainly bought a toy as a reward for using the potty or behaving in a store. In turn, you probably felt rewarded by the smile and hug that greeted the gift, thus compelling you to continue to do it.

Keep in mind, of course, that a "reward" gift isn't the only kind we give our daughters. Almost all major celebrations are focused on gift-giving: birthdays, weddings, Christmas, Hanukkah. Although modern parents tend to decry the commercialism and materialism, it doesn't seem to make a dent in the flow of goods into our houses. Every December (or other major occasion), people pull out their shopping lists, regardless of what the research says they should be doing instead.

Retail Therapy: Only a Short-Term Band-Aid

Even when a celebration isn't occurring, many people look to material goods to give their lives pleasure and meaning, and even to solve problems. In the moment, goods can make us feel better. We work hard to get things and then work even harder to take care of them. We fill our houses and garages with goods of all kinds, and we can't deny that we judge each other—and ourselves—for what we own. We know the things we own send messages, such as we're successful or we have an eye for quality. We ask ourselves, "Is it good enough? Is it hip enough?" And perhaps the most dangerous of all, "Are my objects representative of the 'me' I want people to see?" These are difficult questions to answer, and so the problems mount when we rely on our material possessions to provide meaning and definition to our life.

Now, there's nothing wrong with giving a present or buying something on occasion. I mean, who doesn't love a present, either giving or receiving one? The difficulty comes when the only way we do things is through the giving or receiving of goods. We buy things to show affection, relieve stress, resolve problems, create calm, and diffuse arguments. It's easy to get into the habit of buying things to make yourself (and others) feel better. They do call it retail therapy for a reason: most likely, it's a quick and easy fix to a bigger problem. You turn to shopping to alleviate your own stress and frustration. After another bad day at work, stopping by the department store to buy a new pair of shoes buoys your spirits. It is a much easier solution to managing your emotions than trying to work on ways to make the job you have more bearable and less stressful, or considering finding a new job.

Materialism: the Good, the Bad, and the Ugly

Of course, there are plenty of drawbacks to spending money for reasons like status or stress-relief, including:

1. You end up with less money to spend on other important things, like retirement or a college education.

2. Spending for status or stress-relief doesn't solve the problem in the long-term; you are just putting a Band-Aid on it temporarily.

But the biggest problem with buying into materialism isn't just the damage it does to your wallet. There are more subtle, albeit just as damaging, effects materialism can have on your daughter's growth as a person.

There is no doubt you want the best for your daughter — what's wrong with that? Of course, that is understandable; why *wouldn't* you want to provide her with the best products and opportunities you can? Unfortunately, while giving her the best of everything — the best food, educational opportunities, clothes, and toys — you may be communicating to her that acquisition is the most important thing. Additionally, you may be communicating it is these things that makes one feel proud, accomplished, and happy.

The consequences of a materialistic attitude may affect your daughter in profound ways, possibly ways you have never considered, especially as you assumed that providing her with all the best things and opportunities will insulate her in some way from the negative realities of life. If you continuously buy things simply because you can, you and your children can suffer serious repercussions. You may be:

- Less satisfied with life
- Less happy in all areas of life — work, social, and personal
- Less likely to realize your full potential
- More depressed and anxious
- More self-interested, paranoid, and narcissistic

So, what is the bottom line? If you only seek meaning in things and objects, you will have a very difficult time finding fulfillment. Continuously looking for more things to bring you happiness will only result in the need for a bigger house. Your daughter is watching and picking up on this coping skill. She isn't learning how to manage her emotions in a healthy way, just how to shop them away.

HOW TO REALIGN YOUR FAMILY'S VALUES

It's time to consider what your values are. Determine whether your lifestyle is expressing those values, and you may find you need to make some adjustments. The things you possess send many messages to other people, as well as to yourself. You may even have things that promote your aspirations, rather than your reality. That treadmill in your bedroom, for example, is a fabulous clothing rack, yet you don't want to get rid of it because, maybe *tomorrow* you'll start exercising in the morning before work.

Much of consumerism is automatic. You may not really think about it, and just act on whims instead. Saying yes to a material good is often significantly easier than no, whether it's saying no to yourself or to your children. Saying no means you can feel guilt or regret, or your child may be angry with you. Tolerating these emotions is not easy, and yet it is incredibly important to be able to do. It's even more important to model for your daughter that she can tolerate feeling negative things. Managing emotions in a healthy way is a skill your daughter will use her entire life.

Declutter!

It is very difficult to know where to start to examine how materialism may be affecting you and your life. One sure-fire way to increase your awareness of any of your own material-istic tendencies you may be, inadvertently, passing on to your daughter is to declutter your house. As you sift through the closets, the basement, the garage, and the attic for things you no longer use, clothes your family has outgrown, toys that are no longer played with, and old electronics that have been replaced, you'll get a very clear picture of how much stuff you have, and how much of your life has been invested in getting and storing that stuff.

Include your daughter in the decluttering process. It is a great way to expose her to all of the things she has, and allows her to determine what has value versus what does not. Encourage her to choose where she would like to donate her unwanted or unused things. This is also a great opportunity to promote charity and kindness, wonderful values to instill in your daughter. Brainstorm with her ways to share some of your abundance with others.

Find Out What's Behind Her Requests

When your daughter asks for another X—toy, game, or other object, find out exactly why she wants it. Remind her of all the things you have just gotten rid of. Talk about what you could do instead of buying something, using the real reason she wants the item as a foundation for the solution. For example:

- If she has read all of her books, take a trip to the library instead of the bookstore.
- If she's bored, encourage her to help you create a dinner menu for the week.
- If she's lonely, help her set up a playdate, or spend some time playing with her.

Use her request as an opportunity to teach *creativity* to solve her problems instead of shopping.

Emphasize Experiences Versus Things

A study at Cornell University showed people felt better when they thought about experiences they'd had as opposed to objects they'd spent money on. People think about experiences a lot more than they think about things, and even less-than-perfect experiences get better as they get older, unlike that new gadget, which will soon be outdated and need to be replaced. Experiences, and the memories created by them, do not age, and do not disappear. Here are some reasons:

Experiences Age Better Than Things

Think back to a trip you took. You probably remember the sun shining and the fun you had walking along the beach or riding the carnival rides. You probably don't remember the rain, or all the time you had to spend standing in line—or if you do, it's likely you remember it with a feeling of fondness. But that pair of shoes you bought is still just a pair of shoes. And, if they pinch your toes now, they'll still pinch your toes tomorrow.

Experiences Are Difficult to Compare

In this way, they create far less competition than possessions do. People have a tendency to make social judgments quite often, and will frequently compare themselves with the people around them. If you see the neighbors have a new car, you may feel unhappy, or jealous, until you, too, have a new car.

With life experiences, it's difficult to make hard comparisons and rank them. What's better, a trip to the park, the lake, or the zoo? They're different experiences that can be enjoyed equally. Although you may discuss with your friends how your experience differed from theirs, each of you will have positive things to say about your own exposure to different activities that can be respected and shared.

Experiences Build Social Capital

People may be attracted to shiny new toys, but when it comes to connecting with others, it's through our common experiences that we create deeper connections and relationships. Consider how "the same thing happened to me!" creates a sense of solidarity and understanding, whereas, "I have the same shoes, only in blue," may not be quite as meaningful.

Of course, it's important not to replace a collection of things with a collection of experiences. Collecting experiences as if they were objects and flaunting them in the same way, is still materialism. The goal is not to find a new thing to collect and to parade around as "the best." The goal is to value people, yourself, and the experiences these create, more than the things with which you surround yourself.

Identify Wants Versus Needs

Are you able to determine for yourself what you need versus what you want? We frequently blend the two and do not even realize it. On any given day, you may say things like, "I need a new suit," when the fact of the matter is, you don't *need* it at all. You *want* it. Certainly, you may have valid reasons for wanting it—the old one is out of style, for example. But it is still a want.

One of the biggest difficulties a materialistic person has is separating wants from needs. In our society, a new Dooney & Bourke bag becomes defined as a "need" to the point of making the person who wants it unhappy if she can't figure out a way to get it. It becomes a sad state of affairs when we cannot differentiate between our wants and needs, which then impact our emotional well-being.

When you start being clearer in your own language, you start to see a lot of what your brain thinks of as needs are actually wants, and as such don't have to be fulfilled—or at least not immediately, or not in the way you first thought. For example, your out-of-style suit might benefit from being worn with a few accessories you already own—a patterned top to wear under it, some colorful jewelry, or a seasonal scarf.

In the same way, you can teach your daughter to distinguish between wants and needs, and to not assume the solution to a problem requires replacing something. Sometimes a little ingenuity is all it takes. Model for your daughter how to tolerate the frustration of not getting everything she wants, while teaching her to problem-solve ways to use what she has. This will promote a great sense of accomplishment within her.

Make Thoughtful Choices

Helping your daughter distinguish the difference between needs and wants will go a long way toward helping her be more objective about materialism. That isn't to say a want can't be deeply felt or that it should never be fulfilled. The key is to make well-thought-out choices that are made for the right reasons. What are you really willing to work for, and what might you give up to get what you want? These are crucial questions to ask, and teach your daughter to ask, prior to purchasing anything. Is the trip to Paris worth having to stay at your high-paying but frequently unpleasant job? Is buying the Dooney & Bourke bag worth not being able to buy a latte on the way to work for the next three months? Weighing the pros and cons, which is so necessary to your own decision-making, is an important skill to teach your daughter. Think aloud as you weigh these decisions in your own life so you model the behavior for your daughter.

Another simple, although sometimes difficult, way to help curb materialism is to wait a bit before you purchase whatever it is you have your eye on. You can teach this skill to your daughter, too; delaying gratification is a skill she will need in all facets of her life. Here's how:

1. Create ongoing "wish lists" for you and your daughter. If you stumble across those shoes you *must* have, put them on your "wish list." Add your daughter's "wants" to her list.
2. Sit with the thought of the purchase for a while. Depending on your daughter's age and the item, you could institute a waiting period of a day, a week, or a month.
3. In many cases, the buying impulse will pass, and you or your daughter may find you no longer have a desire for the item. If so, talk about what changed.
4. If after the waiting period ends, you or your daughter still want the item, determine what you need in order to get it. A certain amount of bonus or allowance money? An afternoon spent cleaning out the closet or toy box to donate old items?
5. Once you've met the requirements, if you've decided to buy the item, and have budgeted for it in the appropriate way, then go ahead, make the purchase, and enjoy!

Waiting is never fun, for adults and children alike. Learning how to do it effectively, though, is an important ability to develop, as she will need it throughout her life.

TECHNIQUES FOR DEALING WITH THOSE PESKY MARKETING MESSAGES

In this age of advertising saturation, it is difficult to teach your daughter how to manage consumerism and delay gratification. Everywhere she turns she is being told to buy this now, get this toy first! Marketers are really, really (really) good at convincing us that buying things will confer desirable benefits and solve all of our problems. Who doesn't want all of their problems solved?

Interestingly, studies have shown two unhappy consequences of exposure to advertising for children and teenagers: it increases parent-child conflict and it increases materialistic ideals. In other words, exposure to advertising teaches your child to want things, and to be upset with you when you refuse to buy them, no matter how appropriate your no is.

Television is probably the biggest culprit here. These visual images, with their bright colors and rapid movements, are very persuasive. They catch kids' attention and can keep them spellbound, especially if the people in the commercial look like their lives are vastly improved as a result of that (fill in the blank). In addition to television, radio, magazines, and the Internet all market to you and your child in ways that can make you feel extremely dissatisfied if you don't own X object or sign up for Y subscription. Ads show up on cell phones, in public bathrooms, on the sides of buses or trains, even in schools. Social media is also a big culprit—you can't get away from marketing messages on Facebook and Twitter. In some ways, these are even worse because you can't always tell when someone is communicating a message because they're being paid (or otherwise compensated) to do it or if they're just sharing an experience they've had. We rely on others to help us make decisions about how to get the most value for our money ("Anyone know where the best place to get a new set of tires is?"), so it's easy to be taken in.

Talking about Marketing and Advertisements with Your Daughter

Differentiating between the true message and the gimmick is often a challenge when it comes to teaching your daughter about marketing messages. You can say, "It may seem like it's only an ad about a doll, but it's really trying to tell you that you will have lots of friends and lots of fun if you have this doll. Do you think that's true?" and your daughter may feel, "Yes!" The tough part? She may be right, at least in the short-term.

Living like a hermit isn't a realistic option, and certainly it isn't one that will teach your daughter how to wade through the quagmire of marketing messages. Instead, help her decode them and understand them, and she will be more likely to resist them and will learn how to build positive experiences that don't rely solely on the items she has.

How to Decode an Advertisement with Your Daughter

Children are especially susceptible to advertisements because they don't have the critical thinking skills to identify what is marketing and what is information. Therefore, you have to be the mediator to help your daughter learn to distinguish between the two. Work with your older daughter in the following way:

1. Learn what the messages are in the ads yourself. Look at the advertisements you see critically. What is the superficial message versus the more meaningful one? Keep in mind the underlying message might be far more subtle and yet still powerful. If you start to increase your own awareness, you'll be better prepared to teach your daughter what to look for.
2. Help your daughter learn to identify what is an advertisement. Advertisements appear in highly recognizable ways

(a commercial during her favorite show), and also in some more subtle ways (a show sponsor or product placement in a show). Highlight when advertisements appear. Although they may seem obvious to you, most likely, they won't be obvious to her. Start by pointing out the spots or mentions when you see them to build her awareness. "Look at that! Another ad! Did you see it? Can you see how in drinking Pepsi they are saying *you* should drink Pepsi, too?" Praise your daughter when she correctly identifies an ad. "You're right! That's just someone trying to get you to buy something by making it look terrific."

3. Then, help your daughter figure out the meaning behind the advertisement. Ask questions about who might have put up the ad or made the commercial, and then discuss why people create advertisements. Your daughter may have some interesting insights into why people advertise the products they do. The idea here is to get her to start thinking about things more critically. Although your young children will have a more difficult time with this, you can still start to have some conversations about it.

4. Finally, talk about what the ad wants your daughter to do (buy something). Talk about why it works. "The ad seems to promise you'll have lots of friends if you have this toy. What do you think?" Again, this helps your daughter become a critical consumer. A good consumer is one who thinks about all angles and makes a determination about an item after learning all about it. It is so easy for young girls to get seduced into thinking if they had that toy, they will have many friends and all of their free time will be spent playing and having fun. The reality is far different.

Teaching your daughter to see the message behind the ad will help her to discern what kinds of things she really wants, and help her determine how to build relationships without relying on things to do so.

COMBAT MATERIALISM AS A FAMILY

Though you can't shield your child from ads, you can inoculate her from taking the ad's message too much to heart, and you can help her figure out ways to avoid living a life solely focused on acquisition. The most effective way to help your child learn is to model these behaviors. It's important to really integrate these changes into your way of thinking, and have the rest of your family, especially your daughter, begin to make these changes too.

Express Gratitude for Nonmaterial Things

Demonstrate gratitude for what you are, not just what you have. Show appreciation for who you are, the people in your life, and the things you have to offer, rather than what you own. For example, you can share this with your daughter: "I'm glad my parents taught me how to work hard. It feels good when I accomplish something, like planting that garden, and I like that I now get to share that with you." Open a dialogue with your daughter about what *she* appreciates in her life as well.

Take Risks

One of the reasons people fall into materialism is that it can be a way to feel secure: "If I have enough shoes, I will never have to worry about not having shoes." The truth is materialism does provide a sense of security, albeit a false one. In fact, materialism has a tendency to *increase* anxiety rather than decrease it. It's difficult to maintain a certain level of materialism, and it doesn't provide solutions for managing emotions. It just covers them up.

Instead of acquiring to feed your need for security, take a risk to show you can cope with insecurity. For example, rather than increasing your collection of shoes, go through them and give some away. Notice how you manage okay. Explore what it would be like to get around town without a car to prove if you didn't have one you could still manage. See what happens if you wear a generic T-shirt instead of one from the Gap. Will anyone say anything? And if they do, would you care? Make these experiments fun, and include your daughter. Encourage her to try something new and then discuss how it feels.

Offer Nonmaterial Things

Your daughter almost certainly isn't going to appreciate a certificate good for "ten minutes of real conversation each day" for her birthday instead of that doll she has her eye on, but she will appreciate the attention if you give it to her. In fact, most children do want to "earn" more time with their parents, especially when they are young. Be sure to make the time meaningful: do something fun together, create a craft, or go for a walk. Make sure the time is uninterrupted, which might mean leaving the smartphone at home. Sharing meaningful time with your child goes a long way. Remember, it is the experiences she will remember much more so than that doll.

Be Creative

Have a problem? Look for solutions that don't require shopping. Start out simple and move to the more complex. If you're cooking a meal for dinner and don't have pasta, try it over rice instead of going to the grocery store to get pasta. Fix the hem that has unraveled instead of buying a new skirt. These actions may not seem directly related to combating materialism, but they are! Figuring out how to do with what you have is a wonderful lesson for everyone involved. Creativity is important in creating flexible thinkers and can help your daughter learn ways to manage with just a limited number of items.

It is challenging to undo your own way of thinking, but it is the first step to changing the materialism that may be taking over your house. It starts with you, and then will trickle down to your daughter. If you can start to begin to appreciate the little things, the things that occur every day, such as a pretty flower or a fun exchange with the librarian, and start to promote them, your daughter will start to see the benefit in these things. You may not be able to combat every external message she is overwhelmed with, but you can start to show her they are not the only answers in building happiness and meaning in her life.

THE HEROINE VALUE: PURSUE YOUR PASSIONS

Changing your focus from acquiring material goods to appreciating more interactive experiences is a necessary first step, but making the change isn't always easy to do. Studies have shown materialism is actually avoidance-based behavior. More specifically, research has found people who are materialistic may be trying to avoid bad experiences more than trying to create good experiences. They are moving away from things they don't like and experiences they don't want, and creating a wall of things, instead of moving *toward* those experiences they do want.

It's crucial to understand this, because avoiding pain is different from working to get what you want. They are entirely different attitudes. You first need to know what you want and then believe you can get it in order for this switch in focus to succeed in the long-term.

Think of it as the difference between skipping class because you don't want to take the algebra test (avoiding a bad experience) and studying hard so you can learn, understand the material, and get a good grade (moving toward a good experience).

Which effort is likely to be more successful in the long run? And which effort is more likely to help you accomplish your goals?

That's why the best way to counteract materialism is to help your daughter learn how to move toward what she wants, with "what she wants" hopefully being bigger and more substantial than that new iPod Touch. Encouraging your daughter to develop, and then pursue, her passions will help her become the kind of adult who does what she wants to do, who follows her own values, instead of doing what is popular or focusing on accumulating possessions rather than living a fulfilling life. Again, it's virtually impossible to expect you will never have to buy another gift or you'll never have to wrestle with issues of materialism. However, if you can create balance in your life, and subsequently, your daughter's, the material items will matter less.

AGE-APPROPRIATE SOLUTIONS FOR THE "WHAT YOU HAVE, NOT WHAT YOU ARE" SYMPTOM

It sounds great to start moving in a direction *away* from materialism, but how? Start small. Talk with your daughter about what her areas of interest are which do not involve shopping or "acquiring" something. When she is very young, she may not have the verbal skills to really share with you all of these things, but if you observe her play and the things she gravitates to, you will be able to start to label the ideas for her. If she likes to help you in the kitchen, encourage those behaviors. Ask her to pick out a recipe to make for dinner. Show her how to make the recipe. Teach her how to use what's on hand to make a meal, or have her come up with her own ideas. If she wants to start a lemonade stand, encourage the entrepreneurial spirit, and talk with her about what to do with the money. She may, because it is so easy, want to run to the store and buy that new doll. Talk about options: saving it, donating it, waiting to see what she *really* wants and using it then. The aim is to try to teach some delay of gratification, so your daughter can learn the best way to value relationships, interactions, and ultimately, money.

Ages 2–3

Even when your daughter is this young, she is likely watching a certain amount of television. If you're lucky, she is watching PBS, which has no commercials anyway. If you're like most families, or if she has older siblings, she's also watching non-PBS shows. If she points out something she wants, ask her why. She'll likely have a simplistic answer: "It looks fun!" "Because, I do!" Point out something she already owns that's similar. Tell her about making a list of birthday or holiday wishes to help delay gratification.

If you're the primary caretaker of your daughter at this age, be vigilant about what you're teaching. If you spend your free time at shopping, talking about shopping, or perusing catalogs, she is going to observe this.

Best of all, build in uninterrupted time to engage in enjoyable activities with your daughter. This is a wonderful age to start setting the foundation for teaching her to enjoy meaningful experiences.

Ages 4–5

Now is the time when your daughter starts to make the comparisons of what her friends have versus what she has. She begins to watch more programs that have advertising in them, and starts to get enticed by and vocal about the messages they present. You can begin to help your daughter recognize advertisements and how they work. Support interests she expresses (helping her learn to move toward what she wants), and see if there are ways to support these interests without running to the store.

Talk about how she feels if she cannot have all of the things that her friends have. When she expresses her disappointment, validate that, but don't rush in to remedy it by buying the toy. The earlier she can learn that disappointment is a feeling we all experience, and it won't be the end of the world when we do have it, the better. Learning to tolerate unpleasant emotions without having to cover them up will help her throughout her life.

Ages 6–8

As your daughter continues to grow, and become more social, especially due to participation in school, she will be clearer in the things she likes and dislikes, and the things she wants. As a result of being in school, she is more susceptible to the influences of her peers as well. Since she is also more verbal and able to express her feelings about things, you can talk about how people can have similarities and differences. You can also talk about choices and options. "Mary lives in a bigger house, but her family is a lot bigger than ours." Or, "Mary lives in a bigger house, but her mom says it is really a lot of work. I'd rather have our smaller house and not have to work so hard to keep it clean and orderly."

Your daughter is able to identify and label her feelings more at this age as well, and it is important to encourage her to do so. She may feel angry she cannot have the hot new toy, and that is okay. She is entitled to be upset for not getting what she wants. Take the opportunity to teach her how to express her feelings appropriately and how to skillfully manage them (taking a time-out, taking some deep breaths, crying). If she learns to express her feelings without worry, she will not pursue materialism to navigate her feelings for her.

Combating materialism in your home, while living in a very materialistic society, is no walk in the park. It is challenging to fight the system, yet it is important to get the message across to your daughter there is so much more to her self-worth beyond the things she owns. This message, like so many others, may not be supported outside of your home. However, the more you present it in a nonjudgmental, supportive way, the more likely she will internalize it and take it with her into all of her experiences. If she can disconnect from the importance of the material goods she can have, and connect to the positive experiences she creates, she will develop into a more well-rounded, emotionally balanced young woman.

CHAPTER 5

Earn Your Way

PRINCESS SYMPTOM: Entitlement
HEROINE VALUE: Hard Work

FROM THE BASICS TO THE BEST OF EVERYTHING

When our children are small, they have no way of meeting their own needs—or their wants—without our direct intervention. Whether it's food, shelter, or clothing, they rely on their parents to provide it. That's perfectly natural, of course. Yet you do have to be mindful that *how* you provide these things doesn't turn into entitlement. Your daughter may begin to believe that you (and the world) "owe" her a good life. To an entitled child (or adult) just providing the basics is not enough. The expectation is that you must feed, shelter, and clothe her with the best of everything, and she doesn't think she needs to do anything in return. Oh, and if anything goes wrong? Or isn't *exactly* as she wanted or hoped? That's your fault.

What a tough predicament to be in as a parent. In some ways, especially when your daughter is a teenager, it's to be expected: you cannot do anything right. Unfortunately, this situation is flaring up in girls younger and younger, and it is up to you to change it. Otherwise, your daughter may grow into an entitled person who doesn't know how to take care of herself—and feels free to criticize others for their efforts.

THE PRINCESS SYMPTOM: ENTITLEMENT

Entitlement is the belief that whatever is desired is deserved, just because. There is no understanding that some things are earned rather than owed. Some parents inadvertently teach entitlement by reinforcing that their children are deserving of anything and everything, regardless of how they act or what they do. This goes beyond the basics of healthy food, secure shelter, and lots of love, which of course every child *is* entitled to have.

The entitlement message is further perpetuated by the society around us. How many times a day do you suppose your daughter hears something like, "You deserve X," with X being a new toy, a vacation, a spa day, or some similar luxury? She deserves it! She isn't told, "If you work hard, you can earn these great things!" All she's told is she deserves them. These messages—from friends, family, media—come through to her more often than you can imagine. Spend a day consciously listening for those types of expressions and tally up the number of times you hear it.

An entitled person believes that everything should be taken care of (and everything should go her way), all the time, and if it isn't, she wants to know where to register her complaint. She has a false belief that her needs are more important than the needs of others. This skewed sense of self-importance makes it difficult to find compassion, be kind, or express gratitude. A sense of entitlement can lead to rude behavior, lack of achievement, lack of respect for others, and blaming.

Unfortunately, this sense of "it's all about me" (but not in a good way) can also create a false sense of identity. In some ways, this is the most damaging consequence of all. If a young girl feels as though she is owed everything, and is given everything, she will have a hard time feeling empowered. She does not learn to earn things, does not know how to prioritize her wants, and does not know how to solve her own problems. This could create a life filled with depression, anxiety, a lack of self-control, and a real inability to know how to function on her own, especially because she expects others to do for her what she cannot do for herself.

Of course, parents *should* indulge their children at times. But before you do, consider moderation, think about why you are indulging her, and teach appreciation for the actions you (and others) do, to thwart the development of entitlement.

Learned Helplessness and Disempowerment

Always giving kids whatever they want can teach children they are unable to do anything on their own, and they are "helpless" in making their own way. Helplessness can be a learned behavior. Psychologists have studied this behavior for a very long time, both with animals and people. "Learned helplessness" is a theory which explains what happens when a person gives up trying to do things on her own.

To illustrate this point, there is one study, for example, that showed how an animal would give up trying to get a reward even if the consequences were stopped. A rat's foot was shocked every time it walked across its cage to try to get to food that was set out on the other side. Only by not trying to get the food could the rat avoid the shocks. So, the rat stopped trying to walk across the cage to get the food. Later in the experiment, the shocks were stopped. The rat could have gotten the food without shocks — but it didn't. It had been taught it would get the undesirable consequence so much that it just gave up. What initially was not helpless (the rat) became helpless in the face of adversity.

If you are constantly getting in the way of your daughter's drive to solve her own problems, figure out what she wants for herself, or learn how to work to achieve, then you are teaching her to be helpless, just the same way the shocks taught the rat.

If you provide everything to her, by way of support emotionally, physically, and monetarily, how does your daughter learn how to do things for herself? You are teaching your child to be helpless—you are teaching your child she *is* helpless. If she falls down, and you rush in to soothe her before seeing if she needs your help, she never learns she can soothe herself. She will constantly look to you to regulate her emotions, and will have difficulty figuring out how to navigate them on her own. This could create long-term problems for her in relationships with herself and others. In fact, she may not even be motivated to try to learn it, as she may always try to seek out someone (friends, relationships) to help her regulate herself. In this way, the overindulgence of providing *everything* causes difficulty in your daughter's ability to become self-reliant, and, not surprisingly, can create unhappiness.

When not given the tools to get what they want for themselves, children will:

- Lack self-confidence
- Demonstrate poor problem-solving skills
- Be unable to focus and pay attention
- Feel hopeless
- Have a false sense of identity
- Encounter difficulty realizing their potential

This is partially why children who have grown accustomed to having someone run interference for them react with outrage and fear when they are suddenly held to higher expectations and standards. They don't know *how* to do what they are being asked to do. Someone has always done it for them. Their confusion is displayed as anger.

When you teach your child she does not have to *do* anything to get everything she wants and needs—and she's entitled to it just by virtue of being alive—then you are also communicating the message that she is *incapable* of getting what she wants for herself. This is true for attaining physical things (pouring a glass of juice), achieving accomplishments (studying and doing well on a spelling test), and regulating her emotions (calming herself down after a tantrum). If you mediate your daughter's reactions to things, and soothe her constantly, she will never learn to tolerate frustration, something she will come into contact with throughout much of her life, which will create bigger problems as she develops. This is why you cannot dismiss entitlement as being a harmless form of indulgence.

Your Behavior Sets Her Expectations of Others

Fine, you say—if she won't be able to live her own life, then I'll continue to make sure my daughter has everything she wants and needs—always, even when she's an adult. After all, she's my little girl and she deserves it!

The problem with this approach is people generalize from their experiences. So, if you give your child everything she wants and needs, she is going to expect her teachers, her friends, her boss, and her partner to do the same—and then she'll be shocked when they don't. In fact, she may not even be able to recognize these other people have needs of their own or that she should earn what she wants. She may have few meaningful relationships, because she will not know how to be reciprocal in her interactions. At the end of the day, you will be raising a princess, but not one who will have people in her court. She has potential to be lonely, isolated, and unfulfilled. And those are not things that you can fix or provide for her.

RECOGNIZE ENTITLEMENT IN YOURSELF

It is important to know entitlement exists and you have a hand, as a parent, in overindulging and creating it in your children. But, entitlement is a sneaky creature. You don't always recognize it, so you may not always be able to tell when you're inadvertently creating entitlement attitudes in your daughter. Entitlement isn't just about money and things. Rather it is, most often, about expectations such as expecting a good grade just because you showed up for class—or expecting a promotion just because you showed up for work.

LOOK INWARD

Watch for other signs of entitlement your family may display as well. Maybe you feel this year's vacation will be miserable because you can "only" go to Orlando and not Tahiti. Or maybe having to delay purchases puts you in a bad mood. These are signs you may have a sense of entitlement yourself. Take a step back and look at how you handle things and decide if you have unrealistic expectations or demands of others. If you do, you may have to work on your own sense of entitlement before you can tackle your daughter's.

If you can recognize an "I want" for what it is, you can deal with it in an appropriate way. For example, you can ask if the "I want" is a momentary impulse that will go away. You can ask if satisfying it will take time and attention away from other, more important goals. You can ask if fulfilling the "I want" will only make you feel better in the short-term rather than the long-term. If you find the answer is yes to any of these questions, you may be able to rethink the "I want" and find it easy enough to dismiss: "I want the more expensive car, but buying it means it will take me a lot longer to save for a down payment on a house."

The problem develops because it's very easy to try to justify "I want" with "I deserve." Once you convert "I want" to "I deserve," the thinking process gets disrupted and turns into an emotional situation. If you're thwarted in some way, instead of strategizing other ways to get this thing you want, you may feel angry and upset and blame everyone else for your lack of ability in getting it. "I deserve a new car!" is an emotional response that doesn't mesh with a long-term goal to save for a down payment on a house.

DOES YOUR DAUGHTER FEEL ENTITLED?

Following are some behaviors which may indicate that your daughter is picking up traits of someone who is overindulged:

Whining

A child with a strong sense of entitlement does not know how to take responsibility for her actions, and will look for someone to blame and someone to complain to when things don't go her way. If you teach her that you will solve every problem, she is not going to learn any other alternative than to whine and tantrum until someone fixes it or gives her what she wants. This behavior will likely embarrass you and others around you, and if you reinforce it by giving in, it will continue.

Acting like a Drama Queen

Another potential problem is an entitled child, when things do not go her way, has no framework for assessing the significance of what has gone wrong, and experiences even small problems as major crises. Since she may not have learned effectively how to manage her emotional reactions, a small situation that seems very minor to you gets blown into a huge problem, with your daughter melting down because she has no idea how to begin to problem solve. She has no ability to get perspective, as she has been taught everything revolves around her.

So, rather than using effective problem-solving skills, an entitled child may escalate the drama in unproductive ways. When she earns a poor grade, instead of talking with the teacher about what she could do to improve her grade, she'll complain to all her friends, post snide Facebook comments, and try to get the teacher in trouble with the principal. She is unable to step back and see what responsibility she may have in the situation and how she can become the captain of her own ship.

Playing the Victim

Perhaps even worse than whining about the slights, a child with a strong sense of entitlement may feel like a victim if she doesn't get what she wants when she wants it. Someone who always seeks to blame others for what's imperfect about her life is unable to accept responsibility for her actions and for creating what she wants. She feels "put-upon" in some way and insists that life is unfair, and that everyone is doing this "to" her. Again, there is no ability to step away and see how she contributed to the problem or what she can do to make it different. This idea will be discussed in greater detail in Chapter 8.

HOW TO FIGHT BACK AGAINST ENTITLEMENT

Entitlement knows no boundaries, and is an issue that cuts across all social, racial, and political boundaries. Fighting back against entitlement is not easy. It is challenging to undo things that have been done, and created, in a certain way. To figure out how to resist entitlement, think about what the opposite of entitlement is. Since entitlement is a collection of behaviors rather than just one thing, it makes sense that the opposite of entitlement is also a collection of behaviors that will need to be changed in some way.

Build Self-Control

Self-control is something children need to learn. It's a skill they'll need at school, in friendships, and in most areas of their lives. A person who possesses a strong sense of entitlement may struggle with limited self-control. She wants what she wants when she wants it; she does what she wants to do when she wants to do it. Delaying gratification is not part of the package. Teaching your daughter basic skills of self-control will help her regulate her emotions, manage her wants and needs, and understand the consequences of her actions. All of these things can only help her in the long run. Additionally, learning self-control will help your daughter understand how to deal with the setbacks and imperfections she is bound to encounter in her life.

Develop Focus and Consistency

Stability is something that helps people to succeed in life. Unfortunately, people with a strong sense of entitlement are a lot like butterflies: they flit from one thing to the next without any true or strong sense of who they are and what they want out of life. Today they want a good grade in algebra; tomorrow they want a new dress; Friday they want to have a party.

There's nothing wrong with good grades, dresses, or parties. In fact, these are all good things to want to have. However, these things do not fall from the sky. Effort needs to be put in place in order to achieve them, unless you're planning to use shortcuts like copying your friend's homework and whining to your parents until they buy the dress.

In very young children, it is perfectly natural to jump from thing to thing, idea to idea. In fact, it is to be expected. Young children have short attention spans, and lots of different things catch their attention. Their brains are stimulated by novelty. While that is true, it does not mean you need to (or should) indulge every impulse your two-year-old has. In fact, it's your job *not* to do this. It's important you begin teaching your daughter early that she cannot get everything she wants, and she has to learn to manage her emotions when she does not. The more that you model stability and consistency for your daughter, the better able she is to learn that while you cannot always get everything you want, you can often get the most important things. This is a great lesson that will carry over into adolescence and adulthood too, setting the stage for independence.

Encourage Independence

Independence is a tricky thing. A child often views independence as freedom from parental oversight, rules, and control. They can *finally* do whatever they want without consequences! However, true independence is more nuanced and complicated than that. Independence means you are able to provide for your own needs, emotionally, physically, and otherwise.

There are lots of opportunities to lead by example when it comes to promoting independence. Imagine if your daughter sees you trying to fix the kitchen sink yourself, even though you could afford a plumber to do it. Even if you fail, she is learning a valuable lesson about trying to solve problems yourself. If you encourage her to examine her feelings, and try to sort them out (maybe you sit with her while she is upset without trying to fix the problem), you also are modeling ways she can be independent, especially through learning how to self-regulate. These things are so important, since they teach her she can be in control of her situations should she choose to be. It also teaches her she can take responsibility for herself and her actions. We discuss this more in Chapter 8.

Take Responsibility

Taking responsibility for your actions is difficult, regardless of your age. No one wants to acknowledge when she makes a mistake, when she has to fix a problem, or when she has to make a change. We've all experienced this in our lives. If you've ever wanted to scream in frustration when the customer service rep says, "I'm not authorized to do that," then you know what "taking responsibility" means, and how not doing so can make you feel.

Basically, if you are taking responsibility, you are not blaming others for what's wrong with your life. You are accountable for your decisions and actions, even if it is related to a problem you did not cause. You would not stand up and say, "It's all my fault the river flooded and wrecked my house." That comment doesn't even have any logical foundation. You do have to deal with the problem the flood created, though, and may have to jump right to problem-solving, saying, "The only thing I can control is how I respond to the fact the flood wrecked my house. So here is what I am going to do to start rebuilding."

If your daughter's room is a mess, it doesn't matter why; it just matters that it is. She can blame the mess on the fact her friends were over, played with all of her toys, and didn't help her clean up, and that may, in fact, be true. At the end of the day, though, the room needs to be clean and it is her responsibility to restore it to order. It is your responsibility as her parent to hold her accountable for doing so, and not jump in and do it for her. If she chooses not to do it, think through what the consequences may be and how you will enforce them. She will feel better about her abilities, and herself, in the long run, even though she'll likely be angry in the moment. Work with her to suggest how doing something different next time (asking her friends to help clean) can minimize future problems.

Teach Resilience

One of the most challenging situations for people who live with a strong sense of entitlement is how helpless they are in the face of adversity and how easily beaten down they are when things go seriously wrong.

It is so important to show your daughter how to address head-on the adversity she will encounter, and not avoid it or think if she ignores it, it will magically go away. There are lots of opportunities to model endurance and perseverance for your daughter. For example, let's say you are about to have a difficult meeting with your boss. You have two choices. You can whine, complain, worry, and bemoan the fact your boss is going to be upset with you, that you could possibly lose your job, and express all of these negative thoughts outwardly. Or, you can model for your daughter how to handle situations that can create anxiety in a healthy way: "I'm concerned about this meeting with my boss, so I plan to be as prepared as possible and not expect any particular outcome. If I go in open-minded and ready for anything he tosses at me, I have nothing to lose and can possibly gain something positive. I have no ability to control what happens more than that." In the second scenario, you, as the parent, are taking control of the situation to the best of your ability. You are not hiding, choosing to avoid it, or making excuses. What better example can you set?

Endurance and resilience often go hand in hand. Resilience is an attitude of not letting difficulties get you down; it's continuing to get back up even when the odds are against you. Instead of giving in to frustration, which is so easy to do, demonstrate to your daughter the steps you take to snap back from frustrations. "I was really disappointed not getting that job I wanted, but today I talked to a friend about it, and that made me feel better.

Now I'm going to call a few companies about some other jobs I bet I'd like just as much."

Facilitate Problem-Solving

Problem-solving is not a skill everyone is naturally born with. It really is something that needs to be taught. If you have always gotten what you have wanted without putting forth much effort, and suddenly that is no longer true, you have no idea what to do, and most likely will raise a fuss. We learn early on, during infancy, the more fuss we raise, the more quickly our needs are met. Why should we think that approach won't work as we get older?

It doesn't, of course, which is why it's so important to show your daughter how to solve problems. There are many everyday experiences during which you can do this. Take, for example, a long line at the post office. This is not a big problem, but it is a common one. This is one of those situations in which complaining to management will not likely change the situation for you.

Use this as a chance to model your problem-solving for your daughter: "Well, I don't love this long line, but if I have to come back tomorrow, that means a lot of wasted time. It's probably better to go ahead and wait now. Why don't you tell me what you did at school today?" Or, alternatively, "This line is moving pretty slowly. We may end up being late for the movie. Let's try tomorrow in the morning." Either way, you're modeling an attitude of acceptance, one that is not entitled. Rather than allowing the situation to ruin a mood or a day, you are problem-solving ways to manage it effectively, taking control in the best way possible. You are thinking about how the situation will impact you and the people around you later, and making a good decision based on that. Thinking about what may happen next is a good way to weigh pros and cons and make a choice.

Delay Gratification

Making snap decisions based on emotions can often create bigger problems in the long run. Everyone has heard the phrase "instant gratification." It's related to this discussion in the sense that an entitled person wants what they want *now*, not two years from now. Having the ability to delay gratification is crucial to success and happiness in life. If your daughter cannot figure out how to delay gratification, she may end up in financial trouble, in conflict with people she cares about, and she may not end up getting the things she wants.

This is a difficult skill that even many adults struggle with. They spend their discretionary income on wants and then when there is something that *needs* attention, like the repairs for the car or a leak in the roof, there is no money. Their priorities are not in order, and the message being transmitted is the fun, pretty, exciting stuff is more important than the necessary stuff. If this is how things go in your house, your daughter is learning to place the wrong things at the top of the priority list. She isn't learning that planning ahead brings you more things. She is learning to spend freely, and then get stressed and try to figure out how to manage the negative consequences. See the section entitled "Make Thoughtful Choices" in Chapter 4 for step-by-step instructions on teaching her how to delay gratification.

Teach Her to Think Ahead

Tied in with the ability to delay gratification is the skill of being able to think ahead and plan for what you will need in the future, as opposed to what you need (or want) right now. Just as the cable bill comes due every month, you can expect things will occasionally go wrong and you need to be prepared for that. If you own a car, you can expect it will need maintenance and repairs, so you should set aside some money for this. In the case of car ownership, the specific problem that arises may "just happen"—you didn't expect the timing belt to break on your car three days after the warranty expired, for example—but you can expect a problem will arise sooner or later. Instead of teaching her that bad things fall out of the sky, show your daughter you can anticipate these obstacles and plan for them.

If she notices that you are paying bills, discuss with her what the bills are for and why you pay them, especially things like insurance or mortgages. Talk with her about why you put money into a savings account. Go one step further and open a savings account for your daughter, and start to teach her the importance of financial responsibility.

Help Her Choose Responsibly

Let's say your daughter wants something you don't want her to have. As her parent, you have to tell her no. Take the opportunity to explain why, and let her know you are helping her learn to choose responsibly. While your five-year-old may not appreciate the intellectual side of an argument that ultimately ends with her not getting the toy she wants, you still can explain why certain decisions are being made (in an age-appropriate way), and, maybe even in a way that involves your daughter in the decision-making.

For example, suppose she wants an expensive toy. Instead of just indulging her by buying it, you can help her figure out how to make responsible, wise choices about it. You could say something like, "I know this is something you want. Let's plan some ways that you can get it. You could save your allowance. It would take twenty weeks of allowance to afford it. That's a lot of allowance. Or, you could ask for it for your birthday or Christmas, but then it might be the only toy you would get. Is it really that important to you?" Maybe she will decide that it is not.

Of course, you are teaching responsible choices, and it may just be the toy is unacceptable to you and goes against your values. If the toy is unacceptable for these reasons, you can explain that to your daughter and maintain your stance. She may push, pull, and try to convince you to change your mind. If you are working to decrease her sense of entitlement, and increase her ability to see things as they are, as difficult as it may be to tolerate her negative emotions, stick to your guns and say no.

Develop Objectivity

Objectivity is not something children develop early on. They are very self-focused, and often unaware of how their behavior and actions impact others. An entitled person often has trouble maintaining a sense of objectivity, regardless of age. In other words, everything feels personal. She sees a bad grade not as an evaluation of how she has failed to demonstrate certain skills, but as a personal attack on her. Not getting the ice cream on the way home from school isn't because you don't have time or because you're trying to eat more healthfully; it's because you don't love her.

Being able to step back and see that not everything is "about her" is a skill she will need at many points in her life. Objectivity will also augment her problem-solving skills, because she'll use reason and logic for both. If she's feeling emotionally tied to a situation, it's harder for her to solve the problems that created it. Emotions are not based in logic, and often cloud our objectivity. If your daughter can learn to infuse some logic and objectivity into her problem-solving, she will make better and smarter decisions.

Show Her How to Set Priorities and Make Decisions

We all have come across people in our lives who create situations that are ridiculous, but they expect them to work out regardless of limitations or the reality of the situation. For example, your friend tells you she's planning a trip to New York City, and has decided she wants to spend a week at a luxury hotel in midtown Manhattan, within walking distance of Times Square. She wants to see at least two Broadway shows with great seats, plus do some shopping on Fifth Avenue, and of course she'll eat out every meal. She then follows up by saying she expects to be able to do all of this for less than $1,000 for a family of four, including transportation. Even if you have never been to Manhattan, you know this is an unreasonable goal. Your friend, however, is convinced that it will happen for her.

You think you can provide some insights for your friend, offering the logic that she has missed. However, often you cannot. Your friend knows what she wants, and is determined to find it, but since she cannot prioritize the need, she gets stuck, and ends up never taking the trip, or creates so much debt making the trip ("I deserve the best!"), she has to pay it off for years to come.

In order to fight the entitlement mentality, it's important to understand that tradeoffs are necessary, and are involved in every aspect of life. If you want a high-powered career, you're probably not going to be able to fit it into a twenty-hour workweek, despite your desire to do so. You have to make some sacrifices to get where you want to go.

For a child, you can express this in simpler ways, by highlighting the choices she has within the means that she has. "You have five dollars. The card game is three dollars and the truck is four dollars. You can't buy them both. You'll have to pick which one you want most."

You can demonstrate and discuss this in many other ways throughout your life:

- "To live in a bigger house, I would have to work longer hours, which means I wouldn't be able to do as many things with you."
- "If you stay up late tonight to finish that book, you'll be tired for school tomorrow."
- "If I stay up late to finish this book, *I'll* be tired at work tomorrow."

These are hard decisions to learn to make, but your child will benefit from learning that she does have choices, and often it's how she makes her choices that will help her the most.

Help Her Learn Perspective

Entitled children (and adults) are not solely self-centered, although that is how it feels when you are around them at times. Instead, they do not really know how they fit into the world, or how to fit in the world. They have no sense that their problems (a poor grade) are not crises (a tornado leveled the house) in the scheme of things. Every perceived slight feels like a crisis, and it is up to you to mediate this for your child. Perspective-taking is a skill which develops a little later, and not everyone is good at seeing all angles of a situation.

Teaching perspective, along with gratitude, is an incredibly important step. It's often hard to teach perspective, especially if your daughter lives a life isolated from people and experiences different from her own situation. There are very few opportunities presented to her to give her a sense of perspective. Media doesn't help: Either everything is bigger than in real life (how did the friends on *Friends* afford those apartments?) or so sensationalized ("Stay tuned for the ten things hiding in your house that will kill your children!") as to be impossible to place in a context.

Thus, it becomes important to make a special effort to work on this with your daughter. Try to provide real world opportunities for her to give back. Not only will this help create perspective, it will also help increase her sense of gratitude for the things she is afforded. Keeping her away from these opportunities makes them seem unreal and doesn't allow her to learn how to show compassion. Over the Thanksgiving holiday, see if a local food bank or shelter needs help with meals, and bring your daughter along to participate. During times of crisis in the country, where there may be devastation due to hurricanes or tornadoes, go through your daughter's things with your daughter and encourage her to donate what she does not use. Be open to discussing why this is important and ask your daughter how she feels about it as well. Be sure to really listen to her feelings, and encourage her to continue to express them.

THE HEROINE VALUE: HARD WORK

Giving your daughter what she needs to thrive in life without creating an entitlement mentality is a fine line to walk. You want to provide your daughter with all of the things you possibly can, and simultaneously find ways to counteract the messages she constantly hears that tell her she is entitled to everything she wants when she wants it just for being alive. The most important message you need to infuse is that nothing in life is free (well, almost nothing). Most things are obtained following hard work. Right now, she is relying on *your* hard work to provide her with the things she wants. Ultimately, she will have to learn how to work hard herself in order to be rewarded with the things she desires and to accomplish her goals.

Reward Her Hard Work

Rewarding efforts rather than results has been getting a hard knock lately by pundits who claim that focusing too much on building a child's self-esteem rather than on building a child's skills will lead to dire problems down the road: lack of excellence, inability to compete, rank incompetence, and an inability to handle disappointment, among other negative consequences.

There is some truth to this idea, of course, but you can find a middle ground. The fact of the matter is, when your two-year-old draws a picture, you are not going to critique her inability to use proper perspective or the lamentable lack of realism in the stick figures. You *are* going to encourage her to continue to work hard in order to build her drawing skills, which include having a good pencil grasp and learning form and content. All the while, you are going to praise the effort, too. That isn't accomplished by saying, "This isn't good enough. Try again." It's accomplished by saying, "Tell me about this picture" or "Do you want me to show you what I learned about drawing dogs from my dad?" It is possible (and important) to praise both the effort and the product (the end result).

Although focusing on the end result is important (and a fact of life—no one cares how hard you worked to rebuild the engine if the car still doesn't start), too much focus on it may cause your daughter to tie her sense of self-worth to her grades or another outside measure—which is just as detrimental to her health and happiness as total incompetence would ever be. She'll learn that there are only two options, passing or failing, succeeding or falling, when, in fact, there is a lot of middle ground. In fact, most of us exist in the middle, while we continue to strive to be better.

Build Perseverance

Building up the strength and the "sticktoitiveness" needed to keep moving, to keep pushing, and to keep going, is not easy. You know how this feels. Think about the initial stages of a project. It can be a lot of fun to do when you first start, but eventually you lose some steam and the middle and end stages can be cumbersome and less than fascinating. You can expect your child feels the same way in areas of her life.

We all lose interest sometimes, and there's nothing wrong if she doesn't finish every picture she starts coloring, or wanders off before the building blocks are all stacked on top of each other. The problem begins when this is how your daughter handles *every* situation the minute it gets dull, or challenging, or is not exactly what she expected. Your daughter needs to learn to finish what she starts, and to continue trying even when things get difficult. How can you encourage this? For example, when you're coloring with her and she wants to move on to the next thing, how about saying, "Why don't we finish this picture first?" She may express frustration at having to continue on with something, and an important follow-up question is to explore that frustration. Maybe she isn't happy with how the picture is coming out, maybe she feels like it is ugly, or, maybe she is, in fact, finished with the picture. Don't be afraid to ask the questions and then explore her emotions. Learning to persevere in the face of intense emotions is an important a skill for her to have in her toolbag.

As with all things, you can encourage perseverance by showing her how you do it in your own life. Do you put books down halfway through and never finish them? Do you get halfway through a sewing project and put it away? Does your daughter see you do not finish the things you start? She will make her own assumptions as to why you are not completing projects and may follow your lead, starting and stopping things. As much as we would like to live our lives saying, "Do as I say, not as I do," it's not really an effective method of teaching your daughter how to be the best she can be. So, show her how to take something from start to finish. Commit to complete at least some of these projects as a way to model the behavior for your daughter. Sure, it's easier said than done (who has the time to revisit that sewing project?), but make the effort when you can and she'll get the message.

SHARE YOUR TECHNIQUES

Another good tactic is to mention a time when you felt like giving up but managed not to do so. Be sure to highlight some of the strategies you used to avoid quitting.

One important no-no: when she's in the middle of something, think long and hard before you interrupt her. If you want to build perseverance and then constantly demand your children stop what they're doing to attend to you, you're sending very mixed signals. Sure, dinner is ready—but she only has one homework problem left. Let her finish! This is such an important component. If you encourage your daughter to multitask more than is healthy or stop and start activities constantly, things are bound to get lost and nothing gets accomplished. Promote focusing on one thing at a time in your own life and have your daughter do the same.

Another way to increase your daughter's awareness of the importance of perseverance is to talk with her about people who are good examples of it. Talk about people she knows, celebrities she admires, and yourself. For example, you can mention how her pediatrician had to spend lots of time in school to get the degree she has. Find out how her favorite singer got her big break or how her favorite athlete went pro.

Help Her Build a Strong Work Ethic

Tied in with perseverance, perhaps even inextricably linked, is a strong work ethic. If you want your daughter to develop a strong work ethic, you will need one, too. Making the commitment to something, putting in the effort, and following through, shows your daughter it's possible and you can have a sense of accomplishment at the end.

Be mindful not to give the message that work is everything, though. Your daughter will spot your workaholism before you do, and will believe it's the best way to get positive feedback — that is, to focus on the external rather than in building relationships and experiences with others, especially family.

It can be hard to instill a work ethic in your daughter if all she hears are complaints about work. Many of us complain about our jobs, our bosses, and our paychecks, and we don't necessarily feel there's anything wrong with that. However, if *all* you do is complain — if all your daughter hears about work is how much you dislike it — then you are communicating to her that work is a "necessary evil" and not something that can help you feel fulfilled and happy in life. Be sure to share the positive sides of your job, too. Why do you like working? What kinds of rewards to you get from it? Being a working parent is not easy, but it is a wonderful way to show your daughter she can do lots of things in her life, too.

If your daughter shows industry, praise her for it. When she takes initiative, point it out. When she accomplishes a goal or other achievement, talk about how proud you are for how hard she worked, and how proud she should be of herself. If she doesn't achieve the goal she sets, problem-solve with her about how to change the outcome the next time. Try to be nonjudgmental and open to her feelings. And be aware of the fact you might be more upset about an outcome than she is.

Pursue a Passion Through Hard Work

Sometimes, we choose our jobs simply because we are good at them. Other times, our jobs choose us: it just makes sense for us to follow the path to be a writer, a doctor, a psychologist, a parent. Lifelong interests—even lifelong vocations—can start when a child is very young; that is when the seeds are planted. While it's always good to encourage the exploration of the world, if your daughter has specific interests, support them (within reason, of course). If you can promote her following the path that interests her most, you may be able to help her find her way early, which can bring her confidence and excitement.

In the process, you will be helping her to learn to do the following things:

Focus on What Makes Her Feel Good

Sometimes your daughter will have interests in things where her skills are lacking. That does not mean you should encourage her to find a different pursuit. She may love to dance, and yet isn't ever going to be a student at the School of American Ballet. She can still get a lot of joy out of the pursuit. It also does not mean there are not many other options for her: maybe she will excel at other types of dance, or possibly become a wonderful dance teacher. She may start a foundation for children who want to learn to dance, but cannot afford the lessons. She may have any number of options for turning her interests into something professional for herself. Sometimes, just helping her to think outside the box is the best gift you can provide to her.

Believe in Herself

It can be hard to imagine your little girl as the next big thing, so it's easy to patronize or discourage her. Be careful not to do this. Of course, you may have to provide some realistic expectations for her at times. She may not end up playing quarterback for the Green Bay Packers for reasons outside her control, but who knows? If she has learned a good work ethic, as well as determination and perseverance from you, she may be able to achieve the goals she aspires to. If you discourage the pursuit, you are telling her, directly and indirectly, that she isn't capable. You may even promote the wrong message: that it is easier to quit than to try. Think of how this is going to impact her sense of self.

Help Her Find the Right Environment

If you daughter expresses a desire to play soccer, and there is no soccer program in your town, it may take some work, but try to find a team on which she can play. It's important to support the interest in a way that you can. If she really excels at soccer, maybe you can hire someone from the college team near you to work with her to improve. Tread carefully, however. In an environment that is wrong or unhealthy, your daughter may feel demoralized and lose her passion for the sport. For whatever interest she has, it's essential to find an environment that is supportive and encouraging and that gently pushes your daughter to work hard. One that will crush her spirit is definitely not the way to go. It will create exactly the wrong attitude within your girl.

Teach Her to Focus on What She Can Control

This is a hard lesson for most of us to learn, regardless of age. The world is an unfair place, and for children, it is especially difficult to understand that, and to understand why it is so. Your daughter cannot change the fact the world continues to be unfair, sexist, and racist at times. She cannot fight the fact that people are judgmental and, often make decisions based on false assumptions and incorrect information. In the face of this, what you can do is teach her to be the best she can be and to fight through adversity. She'll need ongoing support from you to recognize how to handle unfair situations, and she'll be able to rise above, accept that life is not always going to be as she wants, and she can still be herself despite all of that.

AGE-APPROPRIATE SOLUTIONS FOR THE "ENTITLEMENT" SYMPTOM

You can help your daughter avoid entitlement by showing her that hard work is the best way to get what she wants. This will help her see she is capable and competent, and she can learn how to do anything she sets her mind to. In addition, you can help your daughter grow up with a positive sense of self and others by following these strategies:

Ages 2–3

Toddlers are learning how to find their way, albeit with you standing beside them. Most of your biggest struggles at this age are going to be over the word "no." The tug of war goes both ways: you can say it, and so can she! Pick your battles wisely, but be aware that you're setting a precedent now that will be even tougher to deal with in the future. So while you will absolutely ensure she has all of the healthy food, secure shelter, and unconditional love you can give her, you also need to be sure you're not indulging her whims just so you don't have to set limits.

If you give in to the tantrums now, your daughter is learning that if she tantrums, she will get what she wants. It is the most basic behavioral principle: reinforce the behaviors you want to increase, while ignoring the behaviors you want to eliminate. The tantrum, because you refuse to buy the doll in the store, is undoubtedly difficult to deal with, unfortunately. But if you reinforce it, it will just continue to happen. It's the short-term win (she'll stop screaming!) but a long-term loss (it *will* happen again). Figure out how to handle your own embarrassment in these situations, which may mean scooping up your daughter and leaving, and keep your wits about you. Saying no, despite the reactions, is a perfectly good answer. The more consistent you are (and ensuring that "no" is not your only answer), the more aware of the world your daughter will be, and the more appreciative she will begin to be for the things that she has.

Ages 4–5

At 4 and 5, your daughter, as she is becoming more social, can better understand the impact of her behavior on others, and how their behavior may impact her. She is still going to make mistakes regarding understanding other people's feelings, but she can be taught to apologize for entitled behavior aimed at others, and encouraged to talk about her feelings of frustration rather than act on them.

This is also a great time to start teaching gratitude to your daughter. Gratitude is an excellent foil to entitlement. If you can start to teach your daughter appreciation, you will help her be happier and more satisfied with her life. Start to talk about things that you are grateful for—make it a routine. Maybe every family member mentions something they're grateful for at dinnertime (similarly to what you might do at Thanksgiving) or maybe it is before bed. Or, talk about three good things that happened during the day. Make a habit of doing this every night so that you begin to bring appreciation into your daughter's life.

Also, at this age, you can be more direct with your daughter about how to prioritize and how to make decisions. Talk with her about how you do this for yourself, and start to guide her as to how she can do it too. Let her try it on her own and see what happens. If it doesn't work, discuss ways to improve in the future.

Ages 6–8

Now that your daughter is in school, you may really start to see the sense of entitlement take hold. While it can be amusing to watch your little diva, and it can seem harmless, do not forget that these behaviors will continue to develop, and, they may not be so cute and amusing as your daughter ages. Be sure you are evaluating what your values are, and you are discussing them with your daughter. She can begin to understand the differences in socio-economics, and it may be time to take her to donate toys, clothes, or time to a shelter.

Continue to teach gratitude to her, to balance the entitlement she may be showing. Research has shown that the more gratitude practiced, the more likely she is to be kinder, gentler, more enthusiastic, and generally more grounded and happy. Work with your daughter to identify ways that she can express gratitude. Help her be creative in ways that interest her (maybe she has some special craft that she would like to make to thank a teacher).

At this age, she may be getting an allowance. Open up a savings account with her so she can begin to learn financial responsibility and how to contribute. Saving is a really important lesson to learn early and often. Maybe, if she wants that special toy, she has to contribute money to purchase it. It will likely help her treat the toy with more respect.

Entitlement is a problem in our society as a whole. We are so bombarded with images that show us how much better our lives will be with this or that object or vacation or luxury, we forget the things that actually make us happiest are positive, honest relationships and experiences with the people around us. If we can build up our arsenals of positive experiences, and those of our daughters, they will be more well-rounded and balanced.

CHAPTER 6

Prize Inner Beauty

PRINCESS SYMPTOM: Surface over Substance
HEROINE VALUE: Being Who You Are

THE INEVITABILITY OF JUDGMENTS

We have all been there, questioning if that woman really looked in the mirror before she left the house, or if that man realizes his shirt and tie completely clash. If you've ever had a judgmental thought about someone who walked into a store wearing dirty jeans and with unkempt hair, you're certainly not alone. You cannot go through life without making judgments; we all do it. In fact, often our snap judgments are the first impression we have about another person. But if you live a life of judgments, and express them, your daughter will, too. Even a subtle facial expression is something she will notice.

The problem is if you rely solely on this initial impression, you miss out on a lot. There's a reason why we are taught, "Don't judge a book by its cover." If you only look at the outside, you never really know what's on the inside. That's because the surface doesn't tell you much of anything about the substance beneath it.

Our culture, in many ways, is based on illusion. Everywhere you turn you are presented with something that may not exactly be what it seems, from literature, to movies, to advertising. Early on in life, we are taught we may have to look deeper into a story to find its true meaning, or to realize the prince is not really the pauper. Our society has a whole lore about not taking things at face value—everything from Aesop's fable of the wolf in sheep's clothing to the story told in *The Great Gatsby*.

Despite the fact you know things aren't always what they appear, you certainly cannot expect to go through life without making judgments based on superficial appearances. But you do have to be aware of when you are being superficial and failing to be open-minded. When you do not bring this awareness to your thinking, you often believe your judgments to be facts, when they may not be based in truth at all.

When Judgments Are Healthy

But aren't judgments good sometimes? Of course—if you're talking about "judgment" as "having insight or intuition about a person or situation." Insight provides information and guidance in your thinking: It is looking at things as they are and perceiving them as such. Intuition is making quick decisions based on similar situations and basic animal instincts. This is actually an important skill to have; in layman's terms, we consider this to be "trusting your gut." Think of all the times this skill comes in handy.

When Judgments Are Unhealthy

Judgments are negative and unhelpful when they involve comparisons of what something is versus what we think it "should" be. "My birthday cake should have been chocolate, and it should have been prettier, and it should have tasted better!"

Judgments are often fueled by emotions, as well. "That man cut in front of me in line! What an insensitive, arrogant, sexist jerk!" Pretty soon, we've spent the morning fuming over the slight and obsessing about what we'll do if we ever see that jerk again.

One key problem with making judgments all of the time, and sticking to them like glue, is they can make you incredibly unhappy! If a judgment is connected to dissatisfaction in some way, and you have the desire for the situation to be another way, you are going to constantly be comparing or wanting change, especially in situations in which you have little control. This situation creates a spiral of unhappiness and discontent. If you look in the mirror and see a short, middle-aged frump instead of the tight-bodied college girl who lives next door, and it creates deep dissatisfaction, you will have made a judgment about yourself that is hard to escape. You can't grow four inches taller. And you can't get any younger. In this way, the judgments you make, especially about superficial things, can wear away your happiness.

Comparing Yourself to . . . Yourself!

Within the field of positive psychology, Martin Seligman found the happiest people judge themselves against themselves ("I'm doing better today than I was yesterday"; "I am wiser now than I was twenty years ago"; "I have a better understanding of myself than I used to"; I can swim more laps this week than last week"), not against others. This is a crucial distinction, and not just because there is always going to be someone who has more/better/newer than we do. It's because you can't make fair comparisons between your life and other people's. You know how you got to be the way you are; you don't always know that about others. If you see that happy couple across the street and seethe with jealousy that your relationship isn't like that, consider that you don't actually have any idea what goes on behind closed doors. You have no understanding of the past that brought the couple to this stage; maybe one went through a traumatic divorce and the other was widowed young—would those really be things you'd want for yourself?

Unfortunately, our first instinct is often to look outside of ourselves to see what is going on with others. This message trickles down to our children, setting the tone for how our daughters will think as well.

THE PROBLEMS WITH SURFACE OVER SUBSTANCE

Clearly, the ongoing comparisons to what others have, what you "should" have, how you or others "should" look, negatively impact how you feel, think, and behave, and ultimately, how your daughter does as well. "Should"-ing doesn't get anyone anywhere.

Chapter 3 talked about how damaging it is to value appearances above all else. There, we specifically focused on body image and the impact of appearances on how our girls feel in their own skin. This chapter takes that idea one step further and shows how focusing on appearances damages relationships. Making superficial judgments about other people can create even more problems in our lives. We may rule out getting to know those we might truly enjoy or we might accept those we should keep at arms'-length, based on solely on the surface rather than getting to know who they truly are—what goes on inside.

Dangerous Assumptions

Valuing surface over substance has the potential to be dangerous. For example, if you think all boys in pressed pants and button-up shirts are "nice" boys, because they are polite to you and look good, you may overlook any negatives the specific boy in front of you has. In fact, you may have a big problem when a "not so nice" guy shows up in the same outfit—the guy who may take advantage of your daughter or swindle you in some way. Sometimes the creeps are the ones dressed the nicest. But if you assume nice appearance equals nice guy, you won't immediately recognize the problem.

Not Learning to Think Critically

Focusing on surface appearances can also impact your use of critical-thinking skills. Taking things at face value means you are not looking to their deeper meaning. You may just accept a situation or person as it is, without trying to understand the motivation for another person's behavior ("Why does he always hang up his cell phone when I walk into the room?"), the reasons for a statement ("Did he mean it when he said he loves me? Does he really act like he loves me?"), or the cause-and-effect nature of a sexy advertisement ("Am I really going to get the hot girl if I buy that car?").

Only looking at the surface limits your ability to question and wonder. In other words, you may mistake a bargaining ploy for sincerity. There's a reason car salespeople always dress in suits and Photoshop is used to make models look so perfect. In the same way, if your daughter is focused only on the surface, this limits her. She will not be able to consider motivations, reasons, or cause-and-effect.

An Obsession with Keeping up Appearances

Another thing to consider is the strain that judging, and investing in, appearance can bring. If everything always has to look pretty from the outside no matter what, that's a sure-fire recipe for financial ruin and emotional distress. If you feel you must keep up with others in an effort to avoid their judgments, you may break your bank—and your heart! Focusing on what you have in comparison to what others have can create an incredible amount of anxiety and frustration, and just trying to keep up can create problems you never imagined.

Be careful of falling into this trap, especially as your daughter is always watching and it will be easy for her to fall into it as well.

It's a Kind of Discrimination

Judging people based on appearance can be detrimental and limiting. In a way, it is a kind of discrimination. Just because that person doesn't look the way you do, or the way you think she "should," she is not someone you want to associate with. That sounds a lot like discrimination.

If you observe someone's differences, but make an effort to get to know the person, and still don't like him based on how he treats people, the opinions he expresses, and actual facts of his character and personality, that is an informed and valid decision. If you simply observe outward differences and just choose to not like him without digging deeper, that is a judgment, unfounded, not based in any kind of fact—and therefore unworthy.

You Don't Value Yourself

Beyond the discrimination component and the limitation it brings, a preoccupation with the superficial can mean you do not recognize your own substance, and possibly you do not value what you have to offer. If you focus only on what you look like, you are not emphasizing all of the other things you possess: wisdom, kindness, humor. You may not do much, if anything, to create a richer inner life and a substantial self. If you don't value your own substance, it's unlikely you value it in others.

This creates a problem when it comes to your daughter, because it is essential for your daughter to know she is more than a one-dimensional character. She is a sum of many parts, with her appearance and her material belongings being only two of the many parts that she possesses. If you do not believe this, however, it's unlikely she will.

You Are Not Your Judgments

There is no way to avoid making judgments. We all do it, multiple times a day. The key is to not get weighed down by them—just notice them, acknowledge them, and let them go before you allow them to impact your decisions or actions. In other words, practice mindfulness. If you can train yourself to do this, you become far less attached to your judgments, and thus, more content and settled. The more "Teflon-like" you are with judgments, the more your daughter will be.

Appearances Are Deceiving

As the saying goes, what you see is not always what you get. Sometimes it is more, and, unfortunately, sometimes it is less.

People often put their best foot forward when you first meet them, and then, when you get to know them better, you realize they are not who they seemed. Maybe you meet someone who is charming and lovely, and then, when you get to know him better, you see his charm is a façade, used to get people to do what he wants. Once you get to know him for a longer period of time, and observe his interactions with others (including yourself) more closely, you realize he isn't really all that charming after all. In fact, he is not very likeable.

Or, you may see a person demonstrate behaviors that, on the surface, appear to mean one thing. But if you take the time to get to know the person better, you can see this is not the whole truth. For example, if you saw a man walking down the street, having a very animated conversation even though he's all alone, your first reaction might be there is something wrong with him. But if you later realized he is talking on his cell phone headset, his behavior would seem normal to you. Once put into context, his behavior makes sense and isn't odd—or even noteworthy—at all.

Or, for another example, maybe you are introduced to someone at a party and she seems cold, aloof, and standoffish. You may decide it is because she does not like you. However, later, you might learn she is just shy and takes some time to warm up. If you had let your initial judgment stand, you could have missed out on having a warm, supportive friendship.

WHEN JUDGMENTS ARE HEALTHY: TRUSTING INSTINCTS

Snap judgments aren't always a bad thing. Sometimes, your gut reactions will be dead on. Our gut instincts provide us with a great deal of information, and in no way should you ignore them, nor should you expect your daughter to do so. Intuition and judgment are different, even though the language to describe them is often the same. As mentioned earlier, intuition is recognizing something as it is, without infusing a lot of other emotion. It's discriminating based on what you see or what you experience, without adding an emotional reaction. Judgment differs from this, as it does add the emotion, which, by causing unthinking reactions, can create more difficulty.

Validate Feelings

That said, intuitive knowing has a definite place in your life. For example, if someone makes you or your daughter feel afraid, then it is important to validate that first response. You do not want to pressure your daughter to be engaged fully with someone who will make her afraid, especially if that is her first, uncensored reaction (and is dependent on her age—a nine-month-old going through separation anxiety is different from a seven-year-old who doesn't like the way her uncle touches her when he hugs her but can't quite articulate why). It is important to validate that the fear (or other emotion) is real. It is helpful, and important, though, to examine what information led to that reaction. This can help you teach your daughter to sort out important from unimportant information ("He has a beard like the bad guy in the movie" versus "She acted like she was going to slap me").

Instinct versus Judgment

While it is valuable to teach your children to recognize their instincts and not to ignore them, you also have to help them understand the difference between instinct and judgment. Of course this is easier said than done; as we all know, it is difficult to differentiate between the two. You want your children to learn that just because someone is different does not mean he or she is bad, weird, strange, scary, or should be avoided. Nonetheless, "difference" can create an anxiety. Letting the anxiety stand unchallenged can lead to avoidance—the child wants to avoid anything different that could make her feel anxious—which will perpetuate the judgments, even if they are unfounded.

It is your job, as the parent, to help your child learn how to minimize her judging (it is going to happen). The goal is to teach her not to ignore her instincts while also understanding different doesn't equal bad. Affirm her instincts when they are on track: "That lady in the movie was sure scary! I jumped, too!" Let her know when another interpretation of a situation exists: "Grandma surprised you when she came in and gave you a hug. You didn't like that because you were playing with your toys. But she was just excited to see you. She didn't mean to upset you." And discuss differences without judgment: "Yes, that boy is in a wheelchair. That just means his legs don't work the way yours do."

Your daughter needs to learn to withhold judgment until she has all of the facts—or at least more of them. Exposure is the first step in starting this process.

EXPOSE YOUR DAUGHTER—AND YOURSELF—TO DIFFERENCES

The more people, places, and things your child knows, experiences, and is exposed to, the better equipped she is to deal with whatever life will toss her way. A wide experience of the world generally means she will be less anxious about how to cope with it. The first time you get on the bus or the plane or the boat is always the hardest.

That's why one of the best, and most effective, ways to help your daughter see that surface is not the most important thing is to expose her to a wide variety of people in a wide variety of settings. This may mean first getting yourself comfortable in these scenarios. Most often, people do not engage in different experiences because they are anxious or fearful.

Anxiety is an incredibly powerful emotion; it can paralyze you and prevent you from exploring your world. If you act in this way, your anxieties and fears will be transmitted to your daughter. If she sees you are afraid of dogs, she will probably be afraid of dogs. If she sees you are afraid to leave the house without looking "perfect," she, too, will learn this is the only way to be. Thus, the behavior you are trying to decrease gets inadvertently reinforced by your own biases.

By the same token, check in with yourself about how you feel about people who are different. If you have your own biases and judgments, these will come across to your daughter. It is important to identify your own fears or concerns about dealing with people different from you, and learn how to navigate them. It is up to you to face your worries and concerns before teaching them to your daughter. She will pick up on your opinions and levels of acceptance. If you want to teach her to be open and accepting, you must be the model for her. This will also open her up to have a sense of moral value of which you can be proud.

If you realize you are uncomfortable around people who are different from you, the best way to fight this is to take a step back and see how often you are exposed to differences. You may not have had much exposure to them in your everyday life, depending on where you live and work. If that's the case, the solution is simple: Start to expose yourself to different things. You will benefit by learning many of your preconceived ideas are incorrect, and you will be in a much better position to help your daughter navigate differences.

As your comfort level increases, begin to open the world to your daughter. The more she experiences, the more accepting she will be of all things, and thus, she will be able to look for deeper meaning in her interactions. Pushing herself out of the comfort of basing all decisions on appearance will help her build positive things in her life.

Where do you start? Find opportunities to expose her to all different kinds of people: the physically handicapped or infirm, the intellectually disabled, people with different religious backgrounds (or none at all), people who are less fortunate, people of different cultures and races. It may not be easy, but be resourceful:

- Look at online calendars and event listings for nearby festivals or fairs that celebrate a particular religion or culture. They often have activities for kids, and you might even be able to sample the culture's dishes, too.
- If she has a classmate who is physically handicapped, arrange playdates so your daughter can see that just because her classmate does not move in the same way, it

does not mean she is any less funny or smart than your daughter is.

- If she has a friend of a different religious background, ask her family if there are any rituals she could respectfully observe to learn more.
- Help those less fortunate. You could begin by donating items from your own home you no longer use, and work up to donating your time and/or money. Look for causes your daughter is interested in, and plan age-appropriate activities.

If you have limited hands-on access to different cultures, races, or religions, find books, programs, and activities that will allow you to learn and teach about them.

EVALUATE YOUR OWN MORAL VALUES

Your understanding of yourself, your likes and dislikes, your biases and acceptances, are what will steer your daughter. The old adage, "Do as I say, not as I do" does not really work in parenting. If you are a judgmental, opinionated person on things that are not substantiated, your daughter will learn this. Prejudices are learned; they are not innate. If you have them, your daughter will, too. If you want to create a different set of moral values for your children, it needs to start with you.

Figure out what is meaningful to you and your family. Do you believe you should treat others the way you want to be treated? If so, this must include all people. You cannot be selective as to whom fits that phrase. If you want to teach substance matters more than surface, you have to practice what you preach; show how respecting others is an important component. Teach your daughter to listen to her intuition, and how to ask questions about her initial reactions. Encourage her to give people the benefit of the doubt at least once. Lead by example.

> ## ACKNOWLEDGE SLIP-UPS
>
> Of course, no one is perfect. Notice when you make judgments based on appearance or acquisition and point them out to your daughter, then talk about why you should not make decisions based on these judgments. Note how ridiculous or unfounded they are and let them go. This will teach her that while we all make judgments, we don't have to act on them or accept them at face value. The more you demonstrate these behaviors, the better able your daughter will understand that people are different but that does not mean difference is bad. Most importantly, she doesn't have to like everyone to accept them. Learning not to focus on superficial appearances will help her be better able to maintain a positive sense of who she is.

THE HEROINE VALUE: BEING WHO YOU ARE

Developing a positive sense of self is great in theory, but so much harder in practice. We all have our moments when we question ourselves, judge ourselves (there's that judging again), and want things to be different. You want your daughter to be her own person, to develop her own inner beauty, and to become a person with her own positive sense of self.

Individuality is something to prize. It comes from developing a strong self and from not worrying about keeping up appearances. Being true to herself and to her convictions will help her grow into a strong, healthy woman.

Unfortunately, "individuality is beautiful" is not always the message your daughter gets. All too often, she gets sent messages that are contrary to this idea. There will be many people—everyone from friends to teachers to television actors to peers—telling her conformity matters more than anything else.

Even you may be contributing to this demand for conformity. If you're embarrassed about your daughter's differences or the way she expresses herself, you, too, are letting her know what she is doing is not okay. In fact, if you've ever thought, "Why does my daughter have to wear everything mismatched? Everyone else's daughter looks neat and put together," and this causes frustration and anxiety for you, you may need to reflect on your own biases and how they may be playing out in your parenting. It is important to allow your daughter the forum for positive self-expression.

Sometimes, even your best efforts will not work. She will be judged by others, and you will have to be there for her to talk about it, help her explore her feelings, and problem-solve how she wants to handle it. If you put your own biases in the mix, she will follow your lead. If you open the discussion up for her to examine her own reactions and ideas, she will be more empowered to be the strong-minded individual you hope she will become, thus setting the stage for her as she develops.

Your daughter will go through many stages filled with many interests. Of course, you do not have to fulfill every whim and fancy she has. You do, though, have to encourage her exploration of all things (even if it's minimally), as long as they are safe. She will learn what she likes and what she dislikes, what she will tolerate and what she won't, and, perhaps, most importantly, how to pick herself up when she gets knocked down. All of these things will make her more resilient, more open and available, and a much more accepting young woman down the road. Encouraging your daughter to be herself and to follow her own path will help her withstand the twists and turns of adult life.

AGE-APPROPRIATE SOLUTIONS FOR "SURFACE OVER SUB-STANCE" SYMPTOM

As with all things, you are the gatekeeper to helping your daughter see there is more to life than appearance. You can help your daughter learn to push beyond that and learn to value what is on the inside more than what she sees on the outside.

Ages 2–3

At this age, you get to run the show (okay, most of the time, at least). Your biggest challenge: Toddlers are based in their emotions and in the moment. They do not possess the logic to mediate their reactions, and will often just follow the feeling they have, whether or not it makes sense to do so. It is up to you to provide reassurance in moments when your child is afraid, and not to push her to do more than she is able. That does not mean avoid situations in which she may be scared. It does mean talking her through it, and providing reassurance and support. For example, not all children like the characters at places like Disneyland or Chuck E. Cheese. Your daughter may be frightened by them. Rather than avoid going to those places, allow her to approach Mickey Mouse in your arms, so she knows it is okay. The less of a big deal you make of it the more she will see it is okay. And, who knows, the next year, she may run up to Mickey Mouse on her own.

Also, do not limit her exposure to things in play. Play is how your daughter will learn about the world and is her primary source of exploration. Do not automatically assume she should play with Cinderella just because she has blonde hair and blue eyes. Allow her lots of chances to explore and experience the world. Provide a variety of toys and experiences that will support this.

The Eric Carle book *The Mixed-Up Chameleon* is about a lizard that wants to become other animals but then learns to accept and love who he is. This can be a good story to read to your child to affirm the importance of accepting who she is.

Ages 4–5

Use her fairytale play to your advantage: talk about how certain characters aren't always what they appear to be. Ask her what she thinks about it, and how she interprets this idea. She is able to share her ideas more now than earlier, so open a discussion, really listening to what she thinks and says.

A wonderful book about a precocious, intelligent girl who wants to keep her individuality is *Big Bouffant* by Kate Hosford. This book supports the message it's okay to be your own person, and be comfortable while doing it.

This is a great age to start to teach about different cultures as well. Find books that talk about individuality, differences, and the like.

Ages 6–8

Your daughter is more influenced by her peers now, especially as she spends more time in school. Encourage her to follow her own interests rather than follow along with the crowd. Do discuss the issues that may arise for her in these situations, though, and validate how sometimes it is difficult to be different.

Encourage your daughter to develop interests that go beyond the superficial:

- Turn off the television and explore the local library or a museum.
- Play a sport.
- Introduce her to a musical instrument.

- Have her help you pick out a charitable cause to contribute to.
- Encourage her to have lots of friends with lots of different interests.
- Expose her to as many different activities, people and situations as possible.

This is a great age for your daughter to explore all the possibilities of who she could become—without limiting herself to a few princess-related stereotypes.

Being an individual in a society that promotes sameness is often a challenge, and your daughter may be pushed to give up her desire to be herself so she can be just like everyone else. This is certainly easier than standing up for herself, so it's up to you to teach her to go beyond appearance and value inner substance over the superficial.

CHAPTER 7

Respect Others

PRINCESS SYMPTOM: Me-First
HEROINE VALUE: Compassion and
Consideration for Others

A BALANCE OF SELF-RESPECT AND COMPASSION

It is important that your daughter be who she is—to express herself fully and without fear—while at the same time understanding how to be compassionate toward others. This is often a difficult skill to build, especially when your daughter is very young and her development dictates her main interest is herself. Developing respect, both for herself and for others, will help her maintain healthy relationships and set reasonable boundaries as she grows up.

You want your daughter to grow up with a healthy sense of self and an ability to look after her own interests while helping her to be mindful that this does not cross the line into the type of "me-first" attitude that translates into aggression and selfishness. It is a very delicate balance and one that you have to start teaching early on.

THE PRINCESS SYMPTOM: ME-FIRST

If you have ever watched kids on a playground for a few minutes, you'll see some of them wait in line to take their turn on the slide while others push past without any consideration. The playground is a great example of how "me-first" can play out in a child's life: The demands to be first, to not share, and to not wait for one's turn show up here just as they will show up elsewhere in life. What your child has to learn is two-fold: that she can't always be first, but neither can she just stand back and let others walk all over her. The line between selfishness and assertiveness is one you have to teach your daughter.

Of course, it is important to pay attention to your child's age. Sometimes, selfish behaviors are simply age-appropriate. Your two-year-old is very self-focused, and not very self-aware. That is to be expected for her age; she hasn't had the chance to even grasp the concept of turn-taking. If the same behavior continues in your eight-year-old, though, it is a different story.

Selfishness may not have lasting repercussions on a playground, but in life it does. Many psychologists believe selfish behavior in young children is a precursor to serious disorders such as oppositional defiant disorder and narcissistic disorder, along with problems managing emotions, depression, substance abuse, or anxiety. While a "me-first" attitude may not end up causing such serious mental health problems, it can lead to other negative consequences as your child develops. Selfishness in children may, over time, lead to anger, controlling behavior, and even violence. It also creates significant stress on families and their communities—such as the classrooms that have to deal with selfish children. As selfish children grow older, they have difficulty establishing—and maintaining—

loving relationships and can become untrustworthy and irresponsible.

It is not enough to understand what may happen later in your child's life when it comes to selfishness, however. You really have to stop and figure out why she is acting selfishly right now. A number of studies have shown behavior, both good and bad, is "contagious" among people. Researchers from the University of California and Harvard Medical School showed that while generosity is transmitted within social groups, so is selfishness. In other words, it is a trait that can be picked up if your child plays with other selfish children. If that's the case with your daughter—she wasn't particularly selfish before she started hanging out with those unruly kids down the street, for example—then you may need to make some changes in who your child plays with or at least limit her exposure and make sure she has the chance to play with less selfish children as well.

Other things that can create selfish behavior in your child include:

- Not providing appropriate discipline consistently
- Spoiling your child for the wrong reasons (to placate your guilt, for example)
- Selfishness is modeled for her and the value of selflessness is not taught
- Something bigger emotionally is going on such as the birth of a sibling

It is so important to step back and think about what role *you* have in creating the selfish behavior, what is learned either at home or in other environments, and whether it is a coping mechanism for other emotions.

Signs of Selfish Behavior

While selfishness shows itself in different ways at different ages and under different circumstances, below are some clear signs your child is having a problem with it:

1. Refuses to help around the house
2. Disrespect to others
3. Acts angry for seemingly no reason
4. Has temper tantrums with family and friends
5. Does not take others into consideration
6. Appears to overreact when things go wrong
7. Expects everyone to bow to her wishes
8. Convinces others to do as she wants
9. Lacks compassion and empathy
10. Fails to recognize others have wants and needs
11. Envies others
12. Talks about herself all the time and lacks interest in other subjects
13. Refuses to take responsibility for herself
14. Is physically abusive toward others
15. Steals things belonging to others

Again, it is important to take a step back and consider the "why" as much as the "what." As you know, sometimes there is more to the situation than what you see on the surface. Other conditions may be setting off what you observe as selfishness. We've all seen or experienced a time when, for example, Joe pushed Bob, and Bob pushed Joe in retaliation, and Bob got into trouble for pushing Joe but Joe never got into trouble for starting it. Bob experiences his punishment as breathtakingly unfair and may not learn anything from it. If the root cause had been determined, then Bob might still have been punished, but it would have been for the right reason: "Even if you are pushed first, the rule is we do not push. You must tell a grownup." Bob is much more likely to learn from that.

Where Selfishness Comes From

Selfishness: Is it an inborn trait or something that develops over time? The truth is, it is a little of both. Infants are naturally the most selfish of creatures. All they want is for their needs to be met—never mind about yours! This behavior is completely age-appropriate—without you meeting your child's needs, your child would be unable to thrive in the world.

Although selfishness is natural in a baby, it is something we hope children outgrow as they learn how they fit in the world and begin developing relationships with others. As your child begins to be more self-sufficient, and able to do some things on her own, you begin to meet some of her needs less and allow her to figure things out for herself. As you do this, your daughter learns there is some sort of give-and-take in relationships. As an infant, she learns this further when she knows being silly can make you laugh, and that, in turn, makes her feel good. Later, your daughter can learn being generous with others can also make her feel good. There are many things that can interfere with this process, though, and it is these things you need to address.

If your child shows signs of selfishness, where does it come from? Here are two possibilities:

Family Members

Children, especially young children, often model behavior they observe. If they have selfish peers, siblings, or parents, they are more likely to develop selfish traits. The difficulty is many children do not realize they are being selfish, especially when they are very young. If adults do not help increase their child's awareness, and step in to curb selfishness, children learn this is the best (and maybe only) way to really get what they want.

Confusing Discipline

As parents, it is easy to accidentally reinforce the behaviors you do not want, while ignoring the behaviors you do want. It is easy to laugh when your daughter snatches a toy from another child in the sandbox, and then not correct her by having her return it and/or apologize for her behavior. If your child wants to please you, and she does, and she knows that a certain behavior entertains you (because it did in the past; you laughed), she will continue to act in those kinds of "me-first" ways. In this way, you are inadvertently encouraging selfishness, and your daughter may begin to think it is okay to act in this way in all situations.

In a manner of speaking, your reactions indulge your daughter, similarly to how you can overindulge her with material things. Although it may seem harmless to let her get away with unacceptable behaviors, just as it seems harmless to buy her gifts (a lot of gifts) for "no reason," these things you are doing will actually encourage her selfishness.

Check in with yourself about what you do. A lack of discipline when your daughter does something wrong will not teach her the sense of accountability needed to combat a sense of selfishness. She will grow up thinking she can act in any way she wants, and will still be cute. She will be in for a big surprise when she interacts with others outside your home.

Knowing how it starts is just the foundation. Knowing what to do to change it—and it is never too late—is, perhaps, the hardest, and most important, part.

The Difficulties in Combating Selfishness

Parents have a very difficult time dealing with selfishness within their own children for a number of reasons:

1. Some parents might be actually displaying selfish behaviors themselves. It is very difficult to change a trait in another person you possess yourself, especially if you are unaware of your own problems with it. It requires a level of insight that is difficult to have, and yet, is so important.

2. Other parents who struggle with this issue in their children are not being selfish themselves, but they do not know how to correct the behavior they observe in their children.

3. Some parents may be more permissive in their parenting skills, and may find it easier to simply ignore the problem and hope it goes away. Parents who are too permissive, and do not follow through with discipline and limit set-ting, will have children who are more selfish than others. Children who grow up with this type of parent will have a hard time *not* expecting others to give in to their every whim; it's the message that has been consistently given to them. Not making discipline a high priority can result in negative outcomes.

4. If parents had controlling, critical, and overly strict parents themselves, they may find it hard to correct their own chil-dren, fearing they will imitate their own parents' failings.

Many of us grow up claiming we will not make the same mistakes our parents made, or feeling as though we will not act as our parents did. While this is a perfectly fine stance to take, it is important to think about what will work in teaching the values you believe in to your daughter and what will not. If you parent in opposition to how you were parented, solely because of that, you may be doing your daughter a disservice, and may make things harder for yourself.

HOW TO HELP YOUR DAUGHTER OVERCOME SELFISHNESS

There's no sugarcoating it: Teaching your child not to be selfish can be unpleasant. No one wants to hear she is doing something wrong; she may throw a tantrum when you start to say no; she may push back, make demands, and have meltdowns. Your child may lash out in anger when her behavior is corrected. This just demonstrates all the more reason for you to stick to your guns on making changes. As difficult as her resistance is, don't let it stop or discourage you. Being aware that it may happen can help prepare you in advance for how you will handle the situation.

The first step in overcoming selfishness is to firmly commit to not tolerating it anymore. If you are really ready to change your daughter's attitude, consistency is the key. You have to start by explaining to your daughter you have new expectations of her behavior, and explain in detail what those expectations are. If you feel the primary change needs to be consideration of others, then make that clear. When you start to redirect behaviors, be careful to ensure you are focusing on the ones that really matter. If your daughter is appropriately doing things that get her what she wants and needs, obviously, you may not need to say anything. It is when she is demanding or solely focused on herself that you need to step in.

Choose Your Words Carefully

When you do respond to an action you interpret as selfish, make sure you speak calmly but firmly. Be sure to keep your anger in check, as selfish children tend to overreact with anger themselves. It's important for you to express your disapproval without yelling or coercing. These behaviors, as you are learning over and over, are transferable. Your daughter will learn that in order to get herself heard, she needs to yell. It is important to continuously point out what behaviors your daughter is doing that may be selfish. The more aware she is, the better able she will be to change her behavior. It will take you letting her know what the behavior is in order to do this.

When possible and appropriate, you can address these behaviors privately to avoid embarrassing your daughter; however, if too long a period of time passes between the behavior and the time you address it, the less likely your daughter will be able to understand what you want and to change the behavior. This is especially true the younger she is.

When you point out your daughter's unacceptable behavior, you do not have to be mean-spirited about it. For example, rather than saying, "Susie, it's very selfish of you to keep pushing past others on the slide. I'm extremely disappointed in you. We're going home right now so you can think about how your behavior hurts other people," you can just say, "Susie, it's Tommy's turn. Remember taking turns means everyone gets to play." Or, pull her aside and quietly say, "I'm worried when I see you pushing people out of the way to get to the front of the line. That behavior is selfish." The more you label the behaviors you want to see change, the more your daughter will know what you mean, and, hopefully, she will start to change those behaviors on her own accord.

Changes to Make at Home

There are many other things you and the rest of your family can do to help shift the selfish behavior your daughter demonstrates. And, as always, it starts with you.

Model Positive Behavior

If you want your daughter to act in a certain way, you must act in that way yourself. It is difficult, because we do often expect children to act in one way while we act in another. Nurture empathy in order to increase selflessness and decrease her selfishness. Empathy allows people to understand where another person is coming from. What better way to combat selfishness? If you can understand another person's point of view and recognize how your behavior impacts him, you will be more giving, open, and caring.

Demonstrate Empathy

Talk with her about how others may feel in certain situations. Help her to imagine what others may feel, so she can learn ways to help or be supportive. For example, ask your daughter how she thinks a new student feels walking into her classroom. Talk about what she might be able to do to help the new student feel more comfortable. Encourage her to think for herself, rather than giving her the ideas yourself. A more in-depth discussion of empathy occurs later in this chapter, in the section called "The Heroine Value: Compassion and Consideration for Others."

Give Your Daughter Some Responsibility

Responsibility can breed respect, and this can transfer over to interactions with others. If she has to treat her things well, she will learn that is also how she has to interact with others. In fact, having responsibility at home will help her see how her behavior impacts others regularly. If she doesn't complete her chore, how does that make it hard for someone else to do his or hers? If you give her chores as a way to contribute to the house, be sure she does them. If this is an expectation in the house, be sure she is capable of completing the chores, provide her with opportunities to do them, and do not pay her for them! Providing payment will actually increase the sense of entitlement, rather than decrease it. Tailor the chores to your child. It is okay that they be simple things, like taking out the trash, cleaning her room, or putting away her laundry. Scrubbing toilets does not have to be the way to teach her selflessness and contribution.

Encourage Gratitude

Raising caring children does not happen by accident. The more changes you make in this way, the more likely you will have selfless children. Although it is a challenging concept to teach young children, gratitude is an important element in making these changes. University of California-Davis psychology researcher Robert A. Emmons has shown in a series of studies grateful people have lower levels of depression and anxiety and higher levels of happiness and optimism. In order to teach this to your child, encourage her to say please and thank you. Teach her about appreciation early. Talk about the things you are grateful for, and help her to identify the things she is also appreciative of. Have her list things that make her happy, and be sure she includes things that are not material.

Insist on Respect and Courtesy

These are two abilities that will help your daughter interact well with others throughout her life, and will help her to express her opinion to others without insisting it is the only one. By modeling how to disagree respectfully, you will teach your daughter how she can register an objection without being rude. Be sure that she sees you acting in this way with adults and children—especially with her! If she can see it is possible to have an emotional reaction, express an opinion openly, and then have a good conversation about it, it will help her to build positive relationships. You can start showing her this at a very young age. When you ask what her favorite color is, and she says, "Yellow!" you can say, "Yellow is a good color. That yellow daisy is bright and cheerful. But do you know what my favorite color is? Blue! It reminds me of the sky." As she gets older, you can teach more complex ways of expressing different opinions respectfully. This skill will also help her to stand up for herself in situations where it is warranted.

AGGRESSION AND LACK OF COMPASSION

Often, when girls do not have the ability to speak their minds freely and stand up for themselves appropriately, they turn to more passive-aggressive, negative ways of interacting. Falling into a "me-first" attitude can actually show itself in aggressive behavior toward others. Selfishness can lead to anger and even violent reactions if the person does not get what she wants. Aggression does not necessarily have to be physical or violent to be, well, aggressive. In fact, girls are significantly less likely than boys to use physical aggression to manipulate and intimidate others. That does not mean their brand of aggression is not as damaging. It is just damaging in a different kind of way.

What Is Relational Aggression?

Girls often use relational aggression to maintain status and to dominate and control others. "Relational" (nonphysical) aggression includes actions such as:

- Excluding others from groups
- Encouraging others to exclude a target
- Teasing, taunting, and insulting others verbally
- Mocking others on social networking sites, or via e-mail or text messaging
- Ignoring others
- Spreading rumors
- Giving and withholding affection to manipulate others

Relational aggression is very powerful and can seemingly come out of nowhere. One day your daughter's best friend is Annie, and the next, Annie is her mortal enemy. Annie may even take it one step further to start rumors about your daughter, impacting her desire to go to school or interact with others.

This is just one way in which relational aggression can play out. In some situations, as in the one with Annie, one girl is the instigator. In another situation, a girl may simply go along with the aggression, for fear of being left out or being the next target. Yet another girl may witness the aggressive behaviors, be uncomfortable with them, but not know what to do about it and so chooses to do nothing. The truth is, the behavior impacts all of the girls involved, and can damage their self-esteem and self-confidence. Whether a girl is the instigator or the target, relational aggression can hurt her ability to form healthy relationships; to build a positive sense of self; and can create many adjustment problems, at school, home and interpersonally.

Although we tend to think of the "mean girl" phenomenon as something that "appears" in middle school and high school, there has been a lot of research currently looking at "Barbie brats" and the fact that relational aggression is starting younger and younger. Psychologists have noted relational aggression in children as young as preschool age! This may seem surprising, but considering that many disturbing behaviors are now appearing in younger and younger children, we can assume that relational aggression will as well. This is all the more reason to start to teach your daughter what it means to have compassion, awareness, and acceptance toward others.

Bullying

Relational aggression is certainly a growing problem in today's society, although it is often overshadowed by stories of more intense bullying. Relational aggression is one form of bullying, albeit considered, historically, to be a milder form. Bullying is defined as a type of repeated aggression that is meant to cause harm to the target. As with most things, it is the repetition of the abuse that creates the biggest problem. Most children can shrug off an occasional slight, but repeated intimidation is a much different matter. Bullying can be verbal (taunting, spreading rumors) or physical (shoving the target into the lockers) or both, and it can happen in person and online.

Bullying is a problem for both the target and the bully. Often we focus on how the victim feels, but the bully's behavior means she is also having difficulties. Bullying is another learned behavior, one that is often passed down. Additionally, a bully may engage in this behavior as a way to feel powerful, when in many other areas of her life she does not.

Children with a "me-first" attitude may be more likely to be the bully rather than the target, especially if they believe their demands should be followed with no regard for others. If a bully cannot get someone to do what she wants, she may bully a peer into doing it.

Many parents know the signs to look for if their daughter is the victim of bullying. It is equally important to be aware of the signs your daughter is the bully. Some signs may include:

- Engaging in physical violence
- Getting into trouble frequently, including frequent reprimands by her teachers or principal
- Blaming others for problems and is unable to take responsibility for herself
- Has competitive streak that causes her to overreact to losing or not doing well
- Is overly concerned about her popularity
- Has friends who bully others

Although much of the media focuses on the impact of bullying on the victim, being the bully has several long-lasting consequences as well. Children who bully others are at an increased risk of developing substance abuse problems, and are more likely to engage in physical violence. Bullies are at greater risk of being school dropouts, and have a significantly higher rate of delinquency than their peers. In fact, those who engage in bullying behavior are at greater risk of going to jail, engaging in abusive relationships, and generally having a difficult time managing their emotional behaviors. You can see, if your daughter bullies others, it is imperative you intervene to help her get on the right track.

Physical Aggression

Physical aggression is a very dangerous way in which a lack of compassion can rear its ugly head. Sometimes physical aggression can occur without the bullying behind it, and other times they go hand-in-hand. Although we assume boys are more likely than girls to engage in physical aggression, it is becoming more and more common for girls to engage in violence in relationships. More often, girls are participating in physical fights, much in the same way as boys have for a long time. Some reports say more than 80 percent of school fights being reported are between girls. Girls fight for many of the same reasons boys do, and also for additional reasons, which are much more based in relationships. Girls may stage fights to get the attention of boys, and while they typically cause less physical harm than boys, they can do significant psychic damage to themselves, as well as to the target. Girls may have a greater sense of guilt following a fight and may feel a larger sense of responsibility following the altercation.

Several factors can cause aggressive behaviors in girls:

- Many studies have shown a direct correlation between television watching and violence in children. Additionally, as a society we are bombarded with violent and aggressive images frequently, and children become numb to it. Television does contribute to this, of course, but is not the only thing that can be considered to be problematic.
- They witness examples of physical aggression in their family. It is important to take a step back and think about how

we teach our daughters healthy ways to handle conflict, and how to stand up in the face of it.

TEACH ASSERTIVENESS RATHER THAN AGGRESSION

Girls are rarely taught to get their needs met in healthy ways. In fact, girls are often socialized to use indirect means to get what they want, instead of stating it outright. If your daughter wants your attention, she may complain of a stomachache, for example, instead of saying she wants you to play with her. If you've ever complained of a heavy workload instead of asking your spouse to help you with the dishes, you know how easy it is to fall into this behavior. But it can lead to relational aggression because you (or your daughter) may find it hard to get your needs met if you only talk about them indirectly. It can lead to resentment and manipulation.

Most girls find direct conflict threatening and will do almost anything to avoid it. They do not know how to manage the intensity of emotions during a conflict with friends. Most girls find it to be a challenge to stand up for their needs while trying to maintain positive relationships because if they disagree with their peer group, or pose a different idea, their friends will not like them or will cut them out. Rather than face being ostracized, girls will avoid the conflict, or be passive-aggressive in their dealings.

It is important to demonstrate what it looks like to have a direct communication, and how to feel confident speaking your mind to the people you care for. If your daughter can see you having these types of interactions, she will feel more comfortable doing it herself.

If she comes to you with a concern regarding a friend, for example, here's how to talk it through with her:

1. Discuss the pros and cons of telling her friend she does not like what is happening.
2. Review what is important to your daughter and support the decisions she makes.
3. When she decides to approach her friend and talk with her openly, you can help her practice what she wants to say, so she feels prepared and ready.
4. Discuss the potential consequences of the conversation, highlighting that her friend may be mad. Talk about how your daughter will tolerate this.

Teaching your daughter how to be direct and how to deal with disagreements maturely will go a long way toward keeping her from using bullying or other negative ways of interacting in order to get her way. In fact, teaching your daughter to have direct interactions may help increase her ability to see others' perspectives and may increase her ability to empathize and have consideration.

THE HEROINE VALUE: COMPASSION AND CONSIDERATION FOR OTHERS

Compassion is so important in combating the issue of selfishness. Studies show children who have strong empathy for others are able to resolve conflicts peacefully, rather than resorting to verbal or physical aggression or violence. Ultimately, you probably want your daughter to learn how to be direct, honest, and caring toward others.

It is important to start teaching these skills early. Teaching empathy starts at home, with your daughter's ability to regulate her own emotions. Again, you should demonstrate how to cope with difficult emotions in sympathetic, problem-solving ways. As your daughter learns how to manage her own emotions, she will be better equipped to understand other people's emotions, and to take their perspectives.

Lead by example. Instead of grumbling about the homeless panhandler on the corner, discuss with your daughter the reasons he may have ended up in that place. Simultaneously, express gratitude that you have a loving family and good health. In this type of scenario, solely handing over money is not enough to teach your daughter the concept of compassion. If that is all she sees, it will actually perpetuate the kind of attitude you are trying to correct. The key here is to display a compassionate attitude and show your daughter what that looks like. If she can see that consistently, she will be able to internalize it and practice it in her own life.

Following are other things you can do daily with your daughter to help her develop the art of compassion.

- Have your daughter take part in activities outside her school and usual friends. Help her find out what she has in common with others she may think are unlike her.
- Encourage your daughter to develop relationships with people of all ages, including adults, who like her for who she is. The more accepted she feels, the more accepting she will be toward others.
- Seize as many opportunities as possible to discuss feelings for other people. Use television, movies, books, and everyday activities to talk about how people may feel in a variety of situations.
- Listen to her without dismissing her hopes, concerns, or fears. Use your own sense of empathy to connect with her. Help her generate solutions to her problems, while also helping her recognize that feelings are okay to experience.
- Show what kindness looks like.

- When you discuss issues such as bullying, go beyond talking about the basics and the facts. Help your daughter identify how she would feel as the victim and the bully and what she might do if she finds herself in either role.

AGE-APPROPRIATE SOLUTIONS TO THE "ME-FIRST" SYMPTOM

While combating selfishness can seem a bit overwhelming, you can take many steps to help your daughter become more compassionate and less selfish. It starts with your attitudes first, of course, but there are other things you can do that will help your daughter understand the reasons why being selfless will build more positive relationships. Starting early, of course, is always the key, although you can implement change at any age.

Ages 2–3

At this age, children don't yet have a framework for putting themselves in someone else's position—they're still figuring out they're independent from Mommy. That doesn't mean they cannot begin to understand basic concepts regarding the give and take in relationships. It is important not to get into a battle of wills, as is so easy at this time. Rather than saying "no" all the time, provide explanations. It is okay to say: "That's mine, don't touch" or "Let's take turns playing this game." In fact, the more you can set clear limits, the more your daughter will understand what the expectations are.

At this age, your daughter can begin to learn to express gratitude by recognizing things she is thankful for. She can begin to see things as separate from her, and identify how they make her feel.

Work concepts of gratitude into your daily conversations. Point out the good things that happen, even when they don't seem good. For example, if the rain prevents you from going to the beach, you can say, "Yeah, it's a bummer that there is rain today, but just think about how happy the plants will be. Soon, we will be able to enjoy them!"

Ages 4–5

Continue to build on your ideas of gratitude that were started at ages 2–3. Children at age 4 or 5 can begin to see beyond just the material items and start to be thankful for friends, family, and positive emotions. Here are other ideas:

- You have probably already been teaching your daughter the idea of please and thank you. Continue to build on that, and have your daughter write thank-you notes. Expressing the gratitude out loud (or on paper) makes it even more meaningful.
- Children at this age can understand the concept of "how would you feel?" although she may need some help in taking perspective. Now is the time to guide her when correcting selfish or aggressive behavior. Ask her how she would feel if her friend grabbed her toy the way she did to him. Allow her to identify her emotions. If she is stuck, provide her with a couple of options (would you feel happy or mad?). Discuss openly how this feeling and behavior might impact her relationships.
- Encourage generosity. Once or twice a year, commit to donating things that are not used to those less fortunate. Involve your daughter in this process and help her understand why it is important.

Ages 6–8

It is at this age that you will see the consequences of the "me-first" attitude the most, if you haven't before.

- Talk, talk, talk. Continue to check in with your daughter about how she feels in her friendships and what she likes and dislikes about her friends. If you notice her friendships are changing rapidly, ask about it. If you are worried because she isn't being open and honest with you, talk to her teacher about what is occurring in school.
- Promote goodwill. She may not be ready to go to the local shelter to serve food, but you can work with her to make a meal for a family in need down the block. Talk about what this means and why it is important to do.
- Monitor your daughter's online activities. Let her know if she chooses to go online, you will be checking what she is doing. She is too young at this age to be on many of the social networking sites, but that does not mean she does not know how to use the Internet and/or send e-mails. Children know more and more about the Internet these days, and may know more than you. Be careful to check her cell phone for activity, if she has one.
- Do not be afraid to say no. She may not like it. She may scream and yell, and it is so important that she learns to tolerate the feeling of not getting everything she wants. This is true in life; it can be true in your home.
- Be patient. This behavior is not going to take hold overnight. She needs to learn it over and over. The more consistent you are, the more she will integrate the idea of compassion into her life.

Changing selfish behavior is a real challenge, especially if your family has inadvertently been promoting it. You now need to be the initiator of the change. If you begin to open up the options to be selfless, express gratitude, and be compassionate, you will find your daughter is well rounded, has more meaningful relationships, and is happier overall.

CHAPTER 8

Rescue Yourself

PRINCESS SYMPTOM: Rescue Me!
HEROINE VALUE: Set High—But
Realistic—Expectations

GOAL-SETTING

Learning to set—and achieve—goals is an important part of
your daughter's development. Identifying the strengths you
hope she will have, and helping her build on them and develop
into an independent young woman is probably your top priority.
We have all met "that woman" who is unable to change a tire,
pay her bills on time, or hold down a job. When discussing her
inabilities, she will explain, "I was always my daddy's princess.
He did everything." Unfortunately, now that she is on her own,
without her father to take care of things, she is at a loss for what
to do or how to handle many situations. So, most likely, she will
look for someone else to step in and take care of her; she never
learns how to, nor does she believe she can, take care of *herself*.

As a society, we would never accept this behavior from a
man at face value. In fact, if we were to witness this type of
helplessness in an otherwise healthy man, we might wonder
about his emotional or mental health. With girls and women,
though, there is a double standard. Rather than expecting them
to be able to take care of these things, we shrug such evidence of

helplessness off, excuse it away, and accept it. What a disservice this does to your daughter if you do not hold her to the same standards toward building independence as you do your son.

While the harm in this may not be immediately apparent (does she *really* need to know how to change a tire?), it can ultimately be very damaging to her if you set such low expectations, and set her up with the belief she needs someone in her life to help her at all times. What compounds the problem is that she is surrounded by the message someone will always come to her rescue. It is presented to her in the media she consumes and then is subsequently reinforced by any people in her life who do not make her take responsibility for her actions, or deal with the consequences of her behavior when necessary. When girls learn they cannot rely on themselves, rather they must rely on others, they begin to learn to be dependent. Dependency means not taking responsibility for yourself, and children first learn this when they are not held responsible for their actions.

THE PRINCESS SYMPTOM: RESCUE ME!

We all need people and support at different times in our lives. We may need to ask our neighbor for help moving some boxes, or for a friend to listen when we feel upset. While we all lean on each other some of the time, co-dependence—whether emotional, financial, or other—in healthy adults creates dysfunction. Someone who is overly dependent on others never learns how to regulate herself, and so she derives all of her positive feelings and beliefs about herself from the outside, instead of the inside. She does not learn how to look internally to sort through her emotions, or how to build on positive things and feel a sense of success. We will discuss this in more detail in Chapter 9, but for now, the important thing to realize is creating a daughter who depends on you to meet her every need, modulate her every mood, and solve her every problem will create more problems and will backfire in the long run.

The Downward Spiral of Dependency

The truth is one type of dependency can lead to other types of dependency, such as using drugs to improve one's mood, using shopping to bolster feelings of self-worth, or engaging in casual sex to feel good. Your daughter will be at risk for viewing relationships as a vehicle for getting what she wants instead of as a means for achieving intimacy and connectedness. A child who is overly dependent on her parents is more likely to wind up in unhealthy co-dependent relationships as an adult. Why? Because she does not believe she can stand on her own and, in fact, she probably does not know how. Being too reliant on others, and not learning how to stand up for herself, can even lead to her participation in dysfunctional relationships that may be abusive and all-consuming. Her fear of being able to manage on her own may make her terrified of losing the person who supplies her needs, and she will be accepting of that person regardless of his or her limitations.

A lot of traits that develop within dependent people only worsen over time, and can impact your daughter in all areas of her personal and professional life. Dependent people often blame others for things that go wrong, avoid responsibility, and complain a lot. Does that sound familiar? It's much the same situation as for a selfish person, discussed in Chapter 7. In other words, selfishness and dependence can be inter-related, and neither quality leads to long-term happiness for adults.

While it is normal for a child to be dependent on her parents — she requires help getting her basic needs met since she can't exactly hold down a job at age three — it is important for parents to encourage their daughter's attempts to gain independence in safe and healthy ways. While fostering a sense of independence, it is equally important to allow your daughter to fall down and have to figure out how to pick herself up. You cannot ride in to rescue her every time things do not go her way. You may have to guide her through the disappointment and problem-solve ways to manage her emotions in the face of it. The key is not to take away the problem or prevent the outcome.

Interdependence is normal; in fact, it is healthy. Humans are a social group; we do need each other. The significant difference between interdependence and dependence (or co-dependence) is that even though we sometimes rely on each other, we still know how to rely on ourselves. If someone is fully dependent on another being, she does not know who she is without that person, and will not be able to make the decisions she needs to make to build a positive life for herself. Helping your daughter learn ways to be self-sufficient will have far-reaching benefits for her as she develops. Her day-to-day activities and life will become richer, and she will be better prepared to handle all of the things life throws at her, all of the social, emotional and personal challenges she will encounter.

Your Worldview May Be Getting in the Way

You have to believe in taking responsibility in order to teach it. If you look to others to solve your problems, make your phone calls, and get you the things you want, you are showing your daughter that someone will always be there to do for her. If you do not start changing this in your own life, there is no way you can expect your daughter to do it.

It is very easy to chalk circumstances and occurrences up to chance, deflect your role in many situations, or even look to a higher power for explanation. While looking to a higher power can be comforting and may provide guidance, it is important to be mindful of how you look to these areas for help, and the message you may be sending to your daughter. Praying for strength or guidance is powerful and helpful, but turning to a higher power expecting it to solve all of your personal ills can be troubling, especially if those things are things you have control over.

SHOW HER HOW YOU MEET YOUR OWN NEEDS

One of the best ways to model independence and responsibility for your daughter is to show her how it is done. That means placing an emphasis on meeting your own needs. It is very easy to put your child's needs first, frequently ignoring your own, giving up things you may want to do in order to please your child. When your daughter is very young, this is a necessary action. As she enters into toddlerhood and beyond, it is important for you to take care of yourself and ensure opportunities to do this. If you do not focus on your own needs, and only cater to your child, you will create stress and frustration for yourself. You may also develop resentment toward your child or your partner as a result of not taking care of yourself. You can only be good to others if you are good to yourself.

The additional pitfall of not taking care of yourself is your children do not see how to create positive and healthy opportunities to get what they need. If they do not see you negotiating with your partner so you can go for a run, take a nap, or do something indulgent, they do not learn this is something they, too, can ask for as they get older. You can tell your child why you're doing what you're doing: "It's important for Mommy to have some alone time so she won't be too tired to play with you." Or, "I haven't had any time to spend with my friends lately so I asked your Mom if she would take you to the park while I play tennis. Next week we can all go together."

Even more important in this scenario: If you give up all the things you want to do, or are able to do, because your child gets upset or tantrums, your child is the one running the show. You are basically showing her if she yells loudly enough, she will be rewarded. This is certainly not a behavior you want to reinforce, and, in fact, is one you want to put an end to as quickly as possible. Children need to learn how to tolerate being told "no," which will also help them figure out how to manage their own disappointment in a healthy way.

THE PROBLEM WITH HELICOPTER PARENTING

It makes perfect sense that you want your daughter to be the best she can be. Almost all parents are anxious for their children to do well in life, and when they suffer setbacks, parents often intervene when they should not. The media has coined a term, "helicopter parenting," that summarizes what this approach does: It keeps the parents constantly hovering over the child's life. Such parenting behavior encourages dependence and discourages initiative and self-reliance. It can make a child feel incompetent; obviously, you don't feel she can handle the problem. It also never allows for your daughter to learn fundamental decision-making and problem-solving skills. If you are always there to clean up the mess and run interference, how can she learn that she has some power over her own life?

Learning to be self-reliant is as much an integral part of the developmental process that brings your child from infancy to adulthood as learning to walk, talk, and dress herself. As an infant, your daughter is completely dependent on you. But by age two, when she's walking, she's taking her first steps away from you and toward independence. She may even be talking about it: "I'm not a baby!" is a common refrain of toddlers. It is her developmental goal at this age to begin some separation from you and begin to explore the world around her. If you discourage your daughter's attempts to gain independence, you are teaching her the only way to be in the world is to be reliant on you. You are not promoting healthy exploration of the world around her, allowing her to fall down and get back up.

ALLOW THE PROCESS TO UNFOLD

As with anything new you teach your children, success will not happen immediately. You will have to take small steps and build on each one as your daughter learns how to rely on herself to get what she needs and wants. Patience is not an easy trait to develop, although when it comes to teaching developmental tasks, it is such an important one to have as a parent. We are patient as our child learns to talk, learns to walk, and learns to dress herself, but waiting for her to learn how to regulate her emotions, deal with disappointment, and take responsibility is not always something we have the patience for.

Often we do this unwittingly, as when we are concerned about safety issues. Of course you want to prevent your toddler from running into a busy street, but letting her loose on a playground to discover and explore at her own pace is healthy and good for her. Additionally, if you jump in every time your child expresses some frustration or takes longer to do something than you would, you not only are damaging her self-esteem, you are teaching her someone will always rescue her when she struggles. Children need to struggle in order to learn how to effectively problem-solve, to build self-esteem, and to understand sometimes they will fail. If you fix it, your child will never learn she can do it herself, and feel the pride that comes with accomplishment. Floating around above her, watching her every move and intervening the moment she has a difficulty might make you feel less anxious, but it does not help your daughter.

Certainly there are times when adult intervention is required, but many times you can and should allow your daughter to deal with the problem. She may need some guidance, which you can give without providing ready-made solutions. When she comes to you with a problem, ask her how she would like to solve it. Discuss the different options she may have, including some you offer. Avoid making one of the solutions that you will take care of it, because she just may say yes. It is important that you let her do the work and handle it herself.

Obviously, if the problem becomes too big for her to manage, you will need to step in and help. If you are providing support along the way, she'll be able to ask you when she just cannot do it, and you'll be able to determine if she's right. Again, if she never fails, she will never appreciate, and internalize, her success. It may mean pushing past your own fears related to her failure, the world, and other situations, that matter most.

Dealing with Your Fears

Fearful parents can create fearful, dependent children who are not motivated to engage with the world because they are paralyzed by their worries. You may feel your fears are legitimate—and many certainly are—but it helps to conduct a reality check from time to time and ask yourself a few questions. What is it you are really worried about? Are your worries justified?

Many common fears are perpetuated time and again that are not actually warranted. For example, many parents have outsized fears of some random stranger kidnapping their child which is one reason they fence their daughters in. Of course, this would be a terrible and terrifying occurrence, but it is also extremely rare—significantly less than mass media would have you believe. It's actually much more common for a child to be kidnapped during a custody dispute or by a friend or family member. In other words, the likelihood of someone walking off with your daughter when you are in Walmart is practically zero. In fact, you may want to focus more on the relationships you already have to ensure you are surrounding yourself and your daughter with positive people. That is much more productive than worrying about the random occurrences that may, or may not, happen and are in any case extremely unlikely.

By the same token, parents worry about the physical safety of their daughters, and worry they may be assaulted sexually or physically. As with kidnapping, most girls and women who are attacked know their attackers. Random physical attacks — whether sexual or otherwise — are comparatively rare. It's not solely the people *out there* about whom you need to worry; you need to be just as concerned — even more so — about the people who are in your life, and in your daughter's life, as they have greater access to her.

Focus on the Prevention, Not the Risk

That is not to say strangers are more trustworthy than friends, or you should encourage your daughter to be friendly to all strangers and to trust unconditionally. That is the other end of the extreme. You want to put risk into perspective and teach her to:

- Be a smart judge of people.
- Learn what it means to build trust.
- Read the signs someone may not be so great.
- Speak up if she is concerned about a person or a relationship.
- Know how healthy people act and interact, how people set boundaries about the behavior of their friends, families, and loved ones, and what you do when someone acts in an inappropriate way.

If she learns from you the outside world is super dangerous and nothing can be trusted, she will be unable to go explore it, and will be that much more dependent on you.

Look Beneath Your Fears

In order to combat some of your fears, spend some time really exploring what they are and why you feel them. Maybe you need to do some research to determine if your worries have validity. It's possible there is a bigger issue under the surface, such as your discomfort with your daughter growing up, and in focusing on your worries you are inadvertently trying to keep her in need of you. Address the underlying reason so you can provide some reassurance to yourself and gain more confidence in letting your daughter connect more fully with the world.

TECHNIQUES FOR TEACHING INDEPENDENCE

As you teach your daughter self-reliance, it's important to highlight her successes and build on them. You can do this by celebrating her victories and then encouraging her to take on even more.

Recognize Competence

In order to promote competence, and continued effort, it is important for you to praise the efforts, even if the outcomes may not be entirely as you wish. As your child moves beyond the complete helplessness of infancy, she becomes more competent in dealing with the world around her. Encourage her to make decisions as to what she wants to do, or how she wants to do things. This can include making a decision about what chore she wants to do first. Fight the urge to jump in and do it for her, even if you see she is making mistakes. While her first efforts may lack polish, recognize her attempts nonetheless. Instead of criticizing what she did wrong, focus on what she did right. "You put all the clothes in the hamper and put all your books on the shelf. Good job! Now, let's see about putting all these Legos back where they belong."

The more you can provide this kind of feedback, the more likely she is to continue to do it. If she does make a mistake, support her in learning what the mistake was and figuring out how to avoid it the next time. The more interested you are in her actions, the more she will participate in the process. Also, the more you encourage her to be involved in the decision-making, the more she will own the experience.

Encourage Decision Making

Once your daughter feels more competent in her life (which is, of course, an ongoing process with a great deal of ebb and flow), you can continue to foster her steps toward independence by encouraging her to make her own decisions when appropriate. One way to start this process is to allow your daughter to make some simple decisions in her life about things you are willing to accept her choices over:

- Present a few options and allow her to select from them. To avoid the endless back and forth which can accompany decision-making in young children, limit the options you present, generally offering only two things from which to choose. For example, ask: "Do you want to wear the red shirt or the green one?" or "Do you want to have a banana or an apple?"
- If she chooses the yellow or the pear, which was not one of the options, and it is available, it is not worth having a battle over. The goal is to have your daughter make a definitive decision and stick to it, while feeling proud and confident in the choice she made.

- Decide whether a bad decision is worth fixing before your daughter learns the consequences on her own. For example, if your daughter wants to go to school without a coat, you can point out she may get cold, but unless there is a true safety issue in play (she has to wait twenty minutes at the bus stop in below-freezing temperatures), why intervene? Point out the possible consequences of her decision, and then let her experience them. If she complains she was cold, you can point out this is a consequence of her decision. You don't need to do this in an "I told you so" way, but in a way that encourages her to consider that information in the future. One of the best ways to keep her thinking about her decision is to ask open-ended questions, such as, "What do you think you could do next time to know if you need a coat or not?"

If you encourage her to do some problem-solving with you, she will feel more empowered and better able to make good decisions in the future. If she has a difficult time coming up with options (depending on her age, she may), you can provide some suggestions without undermining her confidence: "What if we checked the forecast?" or "What if you opened the front door and stood outside for a minute?"

THE HEROINE VALUE: SET HIGH—BUT REALISTIC—EXPECTATIONS

At its most fundamental, dependency is created when you do not have expectations that your daughter can achieve her goals, accomplish worthwhile objectives, or handle problems or challenges on her own. If you keep your expectations low, your daughter will start to internalize the message that she is unable to do more, strive harder, or reach higher.

You're probably not thinking, "I want my daughter to be totally dependent on me well into adulthood!" However, you may have a perfectly ordinary desire to want to take care of her or to help her avoid being hurt. After all, you know more than she does, and you can almost certainly run her life better than she can.

But your daughter *needs* to get hurt, to fail, to face consequences, in order to know what to do to avoid the same experience next time. She needs to know how to pick herself up when she falls. If you don't believe she can do it, you will not set any type of expectation for her success, and your daughter will pick up on this message that says she's incompetent. That's a dangerous message for her to internalize, as it can create a great deal of damage to her self-esteem and confidence.

Unfortunately, it is also a message girls and women get all the time. Media, peers, and even teachers discourage them from believing they can, or should, help themselves in positive ways. We value self-reliant, independent men, but we think of women as connected, social creatures, and we tend to be suspicious of them if they are very independent. If a woman is self-reliant, we often make a lot of negative judgments about her rather than praising her for the ability to take care of herself and to get things done. The double standard has existed for a very long time, and if you do not want to perpetuate it with your daughter, you need to change the way you think, and focus on the positive attributes you want her to have that will afford her similar opportunities to her male peers.

Think Beyond "Women's Work"

It is so easy to pigeonhole your daughter into pursuing typically female-dominated professions, and not push her to do things her male counterparts are doing. Society pushes us in this direction quite often, unfortunately. She will learn from many sources—books, movies, television shows—that certain jobs are "female-friendly." While there's certainly nothing wrong with wanting to be a nurse or a teacher (historically female professions), see if your daughter is aware of what else is available to her. It is your job to expand her awareness to what else she may be able to do or accomplish. She may not realize what other opportunities exist.

If she does not see any examples of a female police chief or a CEO of a media conglomerate, then she is unlikely to consider this as an option and will not know how to take any of the necessary steps to get there. By default, she will be more likely to end up pursuing a stereotypical helping profession, whether or not that is truly what she wants or is good at.

To that end:

- Expose your daughter to all kinds of career options, even from a young age.
- Talk about the very many roles women can play—and have played—in the world.
- Talk about what it takes to achieve important goals—what kind of education and work experience, for example.
- Encourage her to participate in lots of different activities that can expose her to the different options she may have.
- Allow her to play on sports teams with boys, especially when she is younger.
- Do not decide which toys are best for her due to her gender; rather, be open to her playing with anything and everything she may want. Be prepared, though, even as a little girl, she may fall into gender-stereotyped roles during play. Rather than cringe or criticize what you observe, talk about what your daughter likes in these roles and work with her to expand *her* worldview (because, let's face it, her worldview does include princesses and fairies). Help her to see there

are pros and cons in being the princess, and highlight how it might be better to be linked to the heroine in the long run.

Look at All Sides of the Story

So often, society focuses on the superficial aspects of girls, while focusing on the more significant, meaningful aspects of boys. Girls are valued and rewarded for their appearance. Boys are often valued for their intelligence or determination.

Because of this, a pretty girl may naturally end up thinking in terms of being a cheerleader in high school and going to modeling school afterward, especially if she is prized mostly for her looks and not encouraged to focus on more than that. She may see the glamorous side of such a career—having money and admiration, which sounds terrific and exciting.

Unfortunately, she won't see the downside, unless it is pointed out to her, which can include objectification, a short-lived career, focus solely on the superficial, and the like. You do not want to squash her goals and aspirations, and maybe this is really the best option regarding a career for her. You do, though, want to make sure she is making educated decisions and she is looking at all sides of a decision so she makes the best one.

To do that, talk about the pros and the cons. This should be done with respect to any career path your daughter may choose, as there are good things and bad things associated with most careers and most choices your daughter will make. If she decides to go to summer camp, she will miss out on doing things with her friends at home, and yet, she will get to make new friends and have new and interesting opportunities while away. If she wants to be a doctor, going to medical school takes a long time, and will impact her ability to pursue a lot of extra hobbies or avocations. The positive is, of course, she will be a doctor specializing in a field of interest. If she wants to be a stay-at-home mother, talk about the great many benefits to being one, and also mention the level of economic dependence and other downsides that may not be so great.

All decisions have good and bad elements. If you help your daughter observe all of them, you will teach her how to make smart choices, and hopefully will help her to choose the direction that is best for her and will most likely help her achieve the goals she sets for herself. Be mindful not to limit her if you do not have to. The more you encourage her to strive, the more independent she will be.

TRY TO WORK AROUND CERTAIN LIMITATIONS

In talking about the pros and cons of different things, you can also educate her on how certain wants can be met in a realistic way. Maybe she cannot have a pair of Uggs, but she can have a pair of boots from Old Navy that look just like them. She may not be as excited about them, but don't let that stop you from making a poor financial decision. Of course, if she has an allowance and works hard to save so she can contribute to the shoes she wants, why not allow her to get them? She is contributing based on being responsible. Isn't that exactly what your goal for her is?

Help Her Understand What's Realistic

As you discuss choices with your daughter, you'll have to provide a voice of reason, which isn't always fun, but is absolutely necessary. The reason it is so important to point out the possible pitfalls, and not promote a false sense of achievement for your daughter, is that it is up to you to help her form a realistic understanding of what happens in the world around her. She needs to know what it means to make a commitment to something and follow through, without someone coming in to protect her or fix it. By pointing out all sides of an argument, and discussing them with her, she will know what she can expect of you, of those around her, and be prepared for anything that may get tossed her way. She may expect you will provide for her unconditionally, regardless of cost of things, never thinking you have many other expenses beyond just her.

One of the most important jobs you have as a parent is to encourage your children to reach for the stars, while simultaneously recognizing what the limitations may be related to this. What a tough line to walk. You do not want to thwart your daughter's aspirations, and yet, you may observe her dreams are unrealistic and unattainable. Work with her to figure out how to be involved in her dreams and goals in an alternative way, if that's possible. She may not be the best player on her school basketball team, so she most likely will not get to college on a basketball scholarship (and she should probably be made aware of that), but there's nothing wrong with her enjoying the game for its own sake. Even if she's not a math prodigy or won't be solving Unified Field Theory any time soon, she can still find the study of mathematics valuable in relation to other endeavors. Maybe she becomes a math teacher or a computer scientist or an accountant.

Sometimes the best thing you can do for your daughter is help her awareness of her strengths and use them to get where she wants. Not everyone is going to be a nationally-ranked basketball player or a world-renowned mathematician. In fact, the percentage of those in comparison to the "regular" people is pretty small. Tell her that, and help her find ways to participate in the things she loves, while finding the things that will bring her security and a solid foundation. Work with your daughter to identify the goals she wants to achieve and help guide her in sticking to them.

Help Her Help Herself

You want your daughter to grow up believing that with hard work and effort, she can achieve whatever she puts her mind to. If she sets the bar high, and puts the effort forth, she may be able to accomplish anything she wants. Maybe she won't find a cure for cancer, but she can certainly try.

To this end, hold her accountable for her behavior and her actions, and make the goal clear and defined. She needs to know what you expect of her. If you set these expectations early, she will know how to manage herself in the face of them as she develops. If you want her to always do her homework right after school, start that practice as a young girl. As she gets older, she will know this is part of the routine and will, hopefully, start to do it on her own without reminders. Make her aware of the consequences if she does not do what is expected of her.

However, make sure the consequences fit the crime. Be careful not to make a mountain out of a molehill, which can only create a significant sense of guilt or shame within her. This guilt and shame will be enhanced by her belief (based on your reaction to her mistake) she cannot do anything to please you, and depression or anxiety can develop out of that. Rather than be hypercritical and withholding when she makes a mistake (and let's face it, she will make them, just like you do), work with her to come up with some solutions that will keep her from repeating the same mistake over and over. As she gets older, she will be able to problem-solve more effectively on her own. She'll need your help early on in figuring out what to do and what strategies will work, so do not be afraid to help when you can. Just do not always fix the problem for her.

For example, if she's always forgetting her homework, instead of riding to the rescue every morning, or letting her suffer the consequences day after day, help her set out a plan. Maybe this includes doing her homework in the same place all the time, at the same time every day, and keeping a checklist that helps her remember not only what homework she has to do but making sure it gets put in her backpack as soon as she's finished with it. Help her to generate ideas that will work, and ask her if she wants you to help her with reminders or to review the checklist at the end of each night. Sometimes, being independent means recognizing what your weaknesses are. Maybe, for your daughter, planning just isn't her strength. That's okay, as long as she is aware of it and knows how to ask for help when she needs it. In many ways, being able to ask for help, and use it when it's offered, is the best sign of independence.

AGE-APPROPRIATE SOLUTIONS FOR THE "RESCUE ME!" SYMPTOM

You can help your daughter build self-esteem, self-confidence, and self-reliance, all of which will help her as she moves toward independence. Giving her the opportunity to develop competence, educating her on the opportunities available to her, and helping her set high goals are all things that will help her recognize she doesn't have to rely on other people to get what she wants or to solve her problems for her—she can do it herself.

Ages 2–3

Toddlers can start to learn independence; in fact, it is in their nature to want it. Provide choices to your daughter, and accept the ones she makes. Allow her to choose which vegetable she wants for dinner if possible, or which shirt she wants to wear for the day. Encourage her to start to dress herself, and applaud the effort regardless of the outcome. So, she doesn't match and has decided to wear two different shoes. Does it really matter?

Begin at this age to link her actions to rewards. If she learns she can earn something special (and not necessarily monetary) she will be more motivated to do things on her own. Positive reinforcement also helps to increase the likelihood the behavior will occur again. So, if you say, "If you help me put away the clothes, after we're done, I'll play a game with you," your daughter may be motivated to help out, especially if she thinks this is something that can happen other times as well.

Encourage your daughter to express herself and be sure you show her you are interested and involved in the things she talks about. Promote her self-expression.

Ages 4–5

As your daughter gets older, she is more aware of how her actions impact others. Have some open discussions about how your daughter can handle different situations, especially when they do not go her way.

Encourage your daughter to take responsibility for her actions, rather than blaming others when things go wrong. You can say something like: "I know you were mad when David took your ball, but hitting him did not solve the problem and was not the most effective solution. What are some things you could have done instead?" In this way, you are furthering her ability to problem-solve.

Find opportunities for your children to play independently, be it at home or out on the playground. Encourage your daughter to approach other children as they play, and to join in on their fun if possible. Do not hover as she does this, orchestrating the outcome. Sit back and watch it unfold. Talk with your daughter about how it felt to do this.

Ages 6–8

Your daughter, at this age, has more responsibilities overall, both at home and at school. Here is how you can ease her into that workload:

- Help her identify what her "jobs" are and how she will be the best she can be at them.
- Problem-solve with her how she will have time to do her chores and her homework, while still having playdates with her friends. Work with her on when she should ask for help, and reassure her if she cannot do it all, it is okay, and you will help her figure out some solutions.
- Ask her if she wants to be involved in extracurricular activities, and find out what interests her. Support her interests to the best of your ability and, when possible, provide opportunities for her to explore them.
- Have her help with things around the house, and give her certain responsibilities she must do.
- Teach her to be mindful of the time: get her a watch and teach her how to be places on time and in a timely manner. She may not realize how long it takes to get from where you drop her off at school to her classroom, and she may not realize stopping to talk with her friends is what makes her late every morning.
- Talk with her about what goals she has for herself and help her work toward achieving them.

It is much easier, as a parent, to swoop in, clean up the mess, and solve your daughter's problem rather than help her build her own independence. Unfortunately, when you do this, you are not teaching your daughter she has any capabilities. In fact, you are giving her the message she is incapable of taking care of herself or her business. It is your responsibility to allow your daughter to fail, and then help her problem-solve how she can succeed the next time. The more she learns she can get back up each time, the better prepared she will be for her life and the more confidence and resilience she'll have. She'll learn she can trust herself to come to her own rescue!

CHAPTER 9

Create a Stronger Self

PRINCESS SYMPTOM: I'm Only as Good as Others Think I Am
HEROINE VALUE: Personal Empowerment

LOSING YOURSELF

One of the most important things you can teach your daughter is how to believe in herself. It can certainly be a challenge in a culture that pushes for acceptance based on how we look, how physically fit (or not) we are, and what worldly possessions we own. Princess Syndrome convinces girls the only way to know their worth is to rely on what other people think of them. This idea develops out of the ongoing focus on appearance and surface over substance. We all care about what other people think of us and want to put our best foot forward. As a social culture, it is only natural for us to do this. In fact, checking in to see what others think can be very helpful as it provides us, at times, with valuable information.

Unfortunately, this need to look to the external in order to find meaning or acceptance can become an obsession. It may become the *only* way your daughter learns to feel good about herself and it may be the only way she learns about herself, and, in so doing, she may receive a great deal of incorrect information.

The need to look consistently for external validation is damaging to your daughter because it negatively impacts her ability to feel good about herself based on her own inner life. She depends on others to validate her own self-worth. While it is understandable for babies to look to others to validate themselves, the hope is these messages will be internalized and your daughter will be able to validate herself later in life.

WHY VALIDATION IS IMPORTANT

Validation and praise are different and it is important to know how.

What Is Praise?

Praise, which should be offered up as often as possible, provides information based on your daughter's effort or how she pleases you or others. Thus, if your daughter does not do her best or makes you unhappy, then logically this praise may be withheld from her. There is nothing wrong with that, unless it becomes punitive and manipulative.

What Is Validation?

Validation focuses on how her feelings, behaviors, and thoughts make sense given any situation. Validating her feelings provides recognition from you that you really see her: "I can see you are angry I said no." This is, obviously, not the same as praise, but it is equally as important. The more she gets validation, the better able she will be to internalize it and learn to rely on herself for validation as she grows. Your "I can see you are angry I said no" becomes her "I am angry because Mom said no." It is a perfectly natural and perfectly logical process. At this point, she does not need anyone else to recognize or validate her emotion or experience although sometimes someone else may and it could sound like, "I would be so mad, too!"

If she doesn't learn how to validate herself, many problems can arise. For example, always looking to others to determine how she should act or think can lead to co-dependent or enabling relationships, where she is "good" because she is "helping" someone else who doesn't know what he would do without her. It also makes her vulnerable to obsessive and abusive relationships; a textbook definition of a verbally abusive relationship is one in which one partner tells the other what she is thinking and feeling and why she thinks and feels that way. A person who relies on others for her value is likely to feel extremely insecure, to have low self-esteem, and is more likely to suffer from anxiety and depression.

Additionally, if she feels punished or misunderstood by those around her, she may start to question herself, her thoughts, and her feelings. That is a process whereby she internalizes the invalidation of her environment. She may, then, begin to invalidate herself, which can seriously impact her self-confidence and self-worth. In order to feel better, she may engage in risky or dangerous behaviors as a method of coping. More specifically, chronic invalidation of your daughter could lead to self-invalidation, which may only be soothed through engagement in self-injurious behaviors, risky and indiscriminate sex, substance use, eating disordered behaviors, and the like.

How to Emphasize the Difference

Not recognizing your daughter's thoughts, actions, or behaviors early and often has the potential to lead you down this road, especially as she does not learn how to rely on her own awareness and instincts. She looks to others to instruct her, and thus, can be easily misled or invalidated. The fear of losing someone, losing status, or being alone will push her to make some choices you may not like, and yet, may have inadvertently influenced. Validation, affirmation, and acceptance do not mean you have to like everything she does; it just means you still have to like your daughter and teach her to like herself. It is a message you will have to repeat over and over, to yourself and to your daughter. The more she can learn to like herself from the inside out, the better.

THE PRINCESS SYMPTOM: I'M ONLY AS GOOD AS OTHERS THINK I AM

It is impossible to go through life without some sort of external evaluation being sent your way. It starts when we are children and continues into adulthood, where in our places of employment we get our annual reviews, and often a bonus commensurate with how we are performing.

As parents, we constantly subject our daughters to evaluation and feedback: "Your hands are dirty; you need to wash them before we eat." "Your teacher said you pushed Johnny on the playground today. You know that's unacceptable. Tell me what happened and why." "You left the milk sitting on the counter and it spoiled. You have to do a better job of putting things back where they belong."

Even when we ask simple questions—"Did you brush your teeth? Put your toys away? Do your homework?"—they aren't simple questions. They are fraught with hidden messages and meanings our children interpret in their own way, often containing negative undertones, and sometimes their interpretations aren't what we intend. A simple question about homework becomes an accusation about how only some of the homework was done; a question about brushing the teeth implies they were not brushed well; a question about the cleanup of toys includes the unstated assumption the toys were not fully cleaned up.

Rather than ask for information without using a judgmental tone, or even express annoyance or frustration directly ("You said you picked up your toys but they are still scattered all over the floor"), parents often fall into the trap of conveying how they feel through the nonverbal messages they send. A negative tone speaks volumes to your daughter, more so than your words actually do. While she could respond to a direct question or statement, she can't respond effectively to a groan or a tone of contempt.

It is a fine line between encouraging your children to become interested in taking care of themselves, and having them believe that the way to please you is to do so; one way eventually becomes intrinsic (she takes care of herself because she wants to) while the other remains extrinsic (she takes care of herself because it makes you happy). We want our children to care about how they present themselves to the world, but it is very important to make sure the message is clear and straightforward, not filled with judgment and negativity.

For example, if you encourage your daughter to brush her teeth, make sure she understands the reasoning behind it, especially if she does not want to do it. Yet, make sure you explain it in a way that's clear but independent from self-validation. A statement such as, "No one wants to smell your stinky breath" can be interpreted as, "No one will like me if I have stinky breath and it's really important for people to like me," especially if your daughter is dealing with all of the other daily messages that indicate pleasing others and having them like you makes you valuable. If your daughter believes this idea, she will continue to do things for others, rather than herself, and she'll only learn to seek out positive responses. When she gets a negative one, it may shut her down and make her feel bad about herself. The key is getting her to understand how her behavior impacts her first; using the brushing her teeth example, she could get cavities, along with having bad breath, and she won't be comfortable with either.

What Is Empathy?

When you ask your daughter to think about how other people would feel, and if they can see how their behavior impacts others, you're hoping to create empathy: "How do you think it felt when you took Elijah's truck without asking?" It is not such a far leap to understand that having empathy and consideration for others means that they, too, should have empathy and consideration for you.

In learning to care for others, we learn, to a certain degree, others should think about how they impact us and we should care about what they think. Empathy is an important thing to experience, and an important feeling for your daughter to understand. However, it goes beyond an empathic response when your daughter worries constantly about how others think about her, and how much she can do for others to ensure she is liked. It has stopped being empathy when the focus turns back to others' perceptions of her and how she can make sure they like her, and when wanting people to like her is the primary motivation for anything she does.

Certainly the opinions of others matter to some degree: if no one can stand you, you have a problem. For most of us, though, the problem is not that we do not care enough about what other people think, it is we care far too much. In this way, an environment is created in which your daughter believes what other people think and feel about her matters more than what she thinks and feels about herself. As we are aware, the pitfalls of this line of thinking and believing are great, and it is important to teach her it is okay to put herself and her needs first, as long as she does so in a compassionate way that isn't selfish or entitled.

HOW TO HELP YOUR DAUGHTER LOVE HERSELF

Following are techniques for showing your daughter it's okay for her to love her whole self—her feelings, flaws, and strengths:

Value Her for Her

Much of how your daughter learns about herself is reflected in how you see her. You are often the first mirror through which she learns how she is perceived by others. It is important you reflect back to her the positive reflections you want her to see. The more positive information you give (as long as it is true), the more positive things about herself your daughter will internalize.

THE POWER OF LOVE

A very powerful thing you can do is love your daughter—and value her—just for the fact that she is. Not because she's pretty, or nice, or makes you laugh; just because she is. Encourage her to see this for herself. Let her know you value her thoughts and feelings, and encourage her to share them with you. When you do this, you help your daughter learn her strengths and encourage her to recognize them.

The truth is, however, in doing all of this, you also need to be realistic about what you present to your daughter as her strengths and good qualities. If you are not reflecting back to her honestly, she will wonder what to believe and what not to. Children can see through the fake stuff, so try hard not to engage in it. Be honest and realistic. The more you act in this way, the more your daughter will, too. The key here is to look for the good and reflect that back to her, not to try to pretend you see something that isn't there or what you dislike is actually okay.

Don't Withhold Love and Affection

If you're in a phase where you're frustrated or disappointed with your daughter, it's easy to let those feelings play out by retreating and withdrawing affection. It is realistic to expect you will have days when it is hard to be smiling all the time. You are human, too, and your frustrations are as real as your daughter's.

However, if you withdraw every time you are in conflict with your daughter, she will learn one of two things:

1. That this is how you interact with others when something does not go your way, and by extension this is how she should react.
2. That it is her job to fix the problem, regardless of how she feels about it, even though you are the adult.

Certainly, if you are in danger of really losing your temper, taking a self-imposed time-out is a very good idea. Wait until you feel calmer and can handle the situation more effectively before talking to her. However, during the normal slings and arrows of parenting, you have to learn to be able to enforce rules, suffer disappointment, and endure frustration without withdrawing your love, affection, and attention, and making your daughter feel your love is contingent on her compliance. Creating conditions for your love is incredibly damaging to your daughter and will have serious repercussions when she tries to develop relationships with other people.

It is important to separate what she does from who she is. If you work to accomplish this, you will teach her she can make mistakes, and repair them, without losing your love and respect. It's a very important lesson for her to learn, and one she can take into other relationships too. If she knows your love is not contingent on her behavior, she will grow to learn healthy relationships are not either. It also allows her to experience her own feelings fully, and learn to express them in healthy ways.

Teach Her That She Creates Her Own Feelings

Emotions are very difficult things to navigate and we all have times when we do not do it well and we let our emotions rule our responses. The problem with letting emotions run the show is they are not logical, often we are at the mercy of them, and they influence our decision- making in unproductive ways.

When a young child experiences intense emotions, she may feel out of control and in fact, may lose control as a result. When that happens, it is easy to look to others to blame them for what has happened. How often have you heard or said, "You're making me feel bad?" It may feel that way, but it is not true.

The truth is no one can make you feel anything. You are the one who creates your emotions, and you are in charge of them. This is a very important lesson for your daughter to learn from you. The key is to help your daughter learn other people do not cause her emotions, and thus, she cannot get other people to stop causing them. She has to learn how to deal with them — to regulate them — and you can start helping her learn by modeling the appropriate ways to do this. If you blame others or think they are responsible for your feelings, she will pick up on that as a way to cope and will do the same. So, it's important for you to develop a better strategy!

There are some ways to help increase her awareness of her emotions, and learn how to regulate them more effectively:

Step #1: Identify the Emotion

First, teach her how to identify and label the emotion. Sometimes she may not have the emotional language to express how she is feeling, so she may need your help to do so. Additionally, labeling the emotion will help her disentangle it from the person or situation she is having the emotion about. For example, encourage her to say: "I feel sad" rather than "You're a jerk."

Step #2: Distinguish Between Thoughts and Feelings

Second, it is important for her to learn how to distinguish between her thoughts and feelings. Thoughts and feelings, though interrelated, and influential of one another, are not the same. Feelings are feelings, and are valid to the person experiencing them, even if the person experiencing them does not fully understand them and even if an outsider does not think they are appropriate or warranted. ("Why are you crying so hard? It's just a little rain. We'll be able to go swimming tomorrow.")

Thoughts are thoughts, and may not be true. You can challenge a thought ("I am a bad person"); you cannot really challenge a feeling ("I feel like a bad person"). While everyone is entitled to their feelings, and discounting them is invalidating to the person expressing them, you may need to help your daughter challenge her thoughts, especially if they are disempowering or judgmental. Teaching your daughter to accept her feelings, and problem-solve how to deal with them, is incredibly important.

Step #3: Own Your Feelings

Lastly, show your daughter you can take responsibility for your own feelings. Instead of saying, "You are making me upset," say, "I feel upset." While this may not seem like such a big differentiation, it is. In one phrase, you are taking ownership of your own reactions and showing your daughter you can handle it. If you aren't falling apart because you are angry, she will learn experiencing anger is okay. If you recognize your own feelings, you are effectively modeling for your daughter how to do the same.

De-Emphasize Pleasing Others

Most of us find it so easy to just agree with others, and go along with what they say, rather than stand up for ourselves. Your daughter is no different; she is likely to feel this is a better choice than having to risk disagreement or conflict, especially if she is not confident she can handle it.

It may feel easier in the short-term, but in the long-term, she may feel resentful she did what others wanted rather than what she wanted, just as you would feel that way if you always did what other people wanted instead of what you want. People often get caught in this trap because they do not want anyone to be mad at them for going their own way or disagreeing.

Sometimes, the fear of disappointing another person prevents us from taking care of ourselves and we solely focus on how what we do will impact others and how they think of us. If your daughter is always worried about how you will react to her saying what she wants or disagreeing with you, then she is likely to go along to get along. But someone focused on what other people think of her is likely to be overly compliant, and, ultimately she will be overly concerned with pleasing others.

Pleasing others is not the same thing as being loved by them or even being appreciated by them and it is fraught with all sorts of potential downsides. In fact, being a people-pleaser often means putting yourself last, prioritizing other people's well-being over your own, and being unable to set boundaries and say no. Think of how that could negatively impact your life — and consider what it means for your daughter.

Following is a list of the characteristics of people-pleasers. Take a moment to consider what kinds of problems this behavior can create for your daughter if this is the kind of personality she develops.

People-pleasers:

- Do not say what they think or feel but do or say whatever other people tell them to (or think they should say or do)
- Take things personally
- Change how they think and act to make others happy
- Rarely ask for help, because they don't want to put others out, hear "no," or lose someone else's respect
- Value getting along above all other values
- Want everyone to like them

If these are the characteristics your daughter develops, she will base her worth on how helpful she is to others and never learn how to stand up for herself. In fact, she may be hurt by people repeatedly if she thinks by helping or putting them first they will like her more, when, in fact, they will just use her to help them in whatever way they need with limited regard for her as a person. Thus the importance of teaching her to have a voice, and to recognize the people who will want to use her for their own gain, will aid her to stay on the path she chooses without being undermined by others.

Avoid People Who Undermine

There are always going to be people in the world who only feel good if you feel badly. We all know people like this, those who possess the mentality of a crab in a bucket. Instead of observing your determination to get out of the bucket and escape as a positive thing, and possibly helping, or being inspired by your example, the "crab" will do everything to get you back into the bucket, preferring you remain in the same negative place as she is, so that all of you will suffer the same fate, that of getting tossed into the boiling water and served for dinner. People like this exist and can undermine you in many different ways. If they're not holding you back, they are putting you down: Everything they do is bigger or better, prettier or cooler, and they will make every effort to prevent you from achieving you goals by denigrating you or your goals. They may also do all they can to make you feel you are not deserving of success or of feeling good.

For example, suppose you bought a new dress that you love. Rather than offering a compliment (or saying nothing), the "crab" points out an ill-sewn hem or states: "That's not your best color." If your daughter does well on a test, her friend the "crab" will say she did better, or the test wasn't that hard, or her test was more demanding. The "crab" finds fault in everything you do, refusing to take responsibility for her own behavior or actions. She just cannot support you in your success, and is much more comfortable sucking you into her misery.

Just as you need to avoid these people in your life, you need to teach your daughter how to identify them and avoid them in her own. It is important to do this in a nonjudgmental and supportive way. It is easy to say, critically, "Why don't you just stop being friends with Sandy? She's so mean to you." But this stance will put your daughter in the position of defending her friend, rather than seeing how her friend's behavior may not be acceptable and to consider ways to change the situation.

Instead, point out what you observe (without judgment or criticism) and problem-solve with your daughter about what she can do to feel better about the situation. You might say: "You've mentioned that Sandy is mean to you often during recess. How do you feel about that? What would you like to do about it?" In presenting the information in this way, you are helping your daughter control the outcome and teaching her it is okay to feel frustrated. She will learn it is what she does about her feelings that will help her in the end. It is important for you to let your daughter know she always has a choice, even when it does not feel like it or when it is not so easy.

Find a Healthy Way to Value Others' Opinions

Taking control of relationships is not something that most girls embrace. That's because most girls are very socially focused—they want to be sure no feathers are ruffled, everyone plays nicely, and they want everyone to like them. No one wants to be isolated and alone, and yet you do not have to give up your essential self in order to fit in and to get other people to like you.

You want to teach your daughter to reflect on other people's opinions of her, take what she can use, and discard the rest. As tempting as it is, no one's opinion should trump hers; she should never value someone else's opinion more than her own. That is not easy to do, especially if she's surrounded by intelligent, strong-willed, opinionated people. The challenge becomes staying true to herself while respecting others. It's a high wire act, wherein she must balance her feelings and theirs.

Find opportunities to model this in your own life. If your daughter witnesses you having a disagreement with a friend, it is a great moment to show her how it is done. When she asks about it, you can say: "Meghan thinks I should get rid of this bag because it's old and tattered, and she is concerned it might break when I least expect it. She wanted to buy me a new bag for my birthday, even though I do not want one. Although I appreciate that she wants to do that, I told her I really love this bag and I didn't want to replace it now. She thinks that is silly, and that's okay. I'm fine with my decision." In this interaction, not only are you standing up for your wants, you are able to show your daughter you can validate the other person's feelings respectfully and still stay strong on the things that matter to you.

You also must encourage your daughter to consider the things others may say about her, and decide what is important and what is not. She can hold onto the important things and use them to her advantage, while letting go of the unimportant or untrue things. Learning how to differentiate between them is not always easy and may take some trial and error, but it does allow your daughter to learn about perspective taking, an important skill for building friendships and understanding your role in them. "When Joanie told you that you're mean, I think she was upset because you didn't want her playing with your stuffed animals. It's okay to tell people no, but sometimes they don't like to hear it and they may say things that are hurtful in the hopes you will change your mind. As hard as it is to hear her say that, you do not have to change your mind to make Joanie happy." The key element here is to teach your daughter to be true to herself, even if that means facing others' disappointment. The disappointment may be present in the short-term, but the pride and empowerment she will feel is much longer lasting.

THE HEROINE VALUE: PERSONAL EMPOWERMENT

Having a sense of personal power—feeling empowered—is essential when it comes to believing in yourself. At its most basic level, personal empowerment means being able to act on your own behalf regardless of what other people think, say, or do. Of course, this skill develops over time, but it is never too early to start teaching your daughter how to be her own best advocate. Being able to act for yourself, and in your own best interest, is firmly tied to your own sense of self-worth. If you do not think you have the right to speak your mind, then you will not—which is the very definition of disempowerment. If you are constantly changing your behavior to accommodate someone else, that is not acting in your own best interest, either.

In order to feel empowered, your daughter must learn how to value herself. She must learn she has a right to her opinion as much as the next person and she has the right to have her opinion heard, even if people disagree. If she is taught to believe she must be seen and not heard, she will never learn she can get what she wants or fight for herself.

You may be getting tired of hearing this, but it's true: the best way for her to learn this is to observe you doing it. Examine your own sense of empowerment and explore whether or not you feel empowered in your relationships. If you do not, and you are overly concerned with the opinions and feelings of others, now is the time to start to change that. You can discuss your difficulty with this with your daughter, and explain why it is important to act in this way, even while you are learning how to do it yourself. Having a sense of self-worth is fundamental in being able to handle the experience when things do not go your way. If you do not feel positively about yourself, how can you expect your daughter to feel good about herself? If you can't take power over your own life, how can you expect her to take power over her own?

Teach Her to Use Her Feelings as a Guide

The first step toward creating a sense of self-worth is by understanding, acknowledging, and accepting your feelings, including negative ones. If you discourage your daughter from expressing—or even having—feelings, especially negative ones, she cannot truly learn to live an authentic life. She needs to be able to experience all of her feelings and use them as a guide. If certain relationships make her angry or unhappy, she needs to use those feelings to help her figure out that the relationship may not be in her best interest, or at the least needs to be changed somehow.

If she knows that she would be happy doing certain activities, then letting those feelings guide her choices empowers her to live the life that will make her happy and fulfilled. Although feelings may have no apparent logic, when one stops and considers them, they do make sense. Teach your daughter to be a detective into her feelings. Encourage her to ask herself why she feels a certain way. It may be difficult for her to identify, but help her think about her feelings so she really starts to understand them. After she is able to determine why she has a feeling in the first place, she can decide what she wants to do about it. This process will help her make more appropriate decisions, not ones that are motivated and informed solely by her emotions, which may lead her to make choices that are irreversible, and that she may regret. Instead, she will learn to make decisions that are based on good judgment, but are guided by how she feels about her experiences.

Teach People How to Treat Her

There is a saying that we teach people how to treat us. By the same token, you teach others how to treat your daughter by the way you treat her. If you never listen to your daughter's opinion, you are teaching her that her opinion does not count, and therefore she will not expect others to consider her opinion important. In effect, you are silencing her voice, even if that is not your intention. Encourage your daughter to express herself, and listen to what she has to say. Show her you are interested, which means looking at her, making eye contact, and paying attention. Address her by name, which shows you have some respect for her. Teach her how to have interactions that may include conflict, and can still be respectful. The more you treat her with respect, the greater the likelihood she will respect herself and others will too.

Show Her How to Set Boundaries—and Respect Hers

When your daughter is very young, she doesn't fully understand you're a separate person. She hasn't differentiated herself from you, and, most likely, she will not until she hits toddlerhood. As she begins to see there is a life outside of you, one she can explore on her own, it is up to you to teach her what boundaries exist. Initially, this may relate to physical boundaries, such as not running into the street. Over time, it will broaden into interpersonal boundaries as well, such as she is not allowed to reach down your shirt or just hug any stranger she sees.

When she's old enough, explain to her it is okay for *her* to have boundaries and to set limits, just as it is okay for you to have boundaries and to set limits. Discuss with her the boundaries you have for yourself and for others (within reason and in age-appropriate ways) and how these boundaries can change as relationships change. You have different boundaries for someone you don't know than for someone you do; you have different boundaries for someone you've known for a long time and have grown to trust, as compared to someone you are just getting to know.

Explain in ways she can understand: "I let my sister borrow my car because I know she will be very careful with it, but I don't know the next-door neighbor well enough to be sure she would do the same." Or, "Grandma is allowed to pick you up from school because she's your grandma. Even though we like Mike a lot, he isn't allowed to pick you up from school because we only met him a few weeks ago."

As you discuss your boundaries and limitations with your daughter, begin to explore what types of limits she has. This should not be a one-time conversation. It must start early and continue on as she develops, especially into her teenage years. Once she starts to identify what her boundaries are, be sure to respect them, as long as they are safe—"No parents are allowed in my room" is an inappropriate boundary. Do not ridicule the things she may present, no matter how silly some of them may seem ("No one is allowed to touch my stuffed animals but me!"). It will help her to feel respected if you actually *do* respect her wishes. If she feels she needs a time-out from you, allow her to take it. If she is uncomfortable playing with the boy down the street, but you are friends with his mother, honor her request not to play with him and find time to spend with your friend when it does not impact your daughter in a negative way. The more you listen and respond, the better able she will be to set boundaries (and respect others') in all areas of her life—with friends, with family, and, most importantly, with herself.

Encourage Her to Develop a Relationship with Herself

Most Americans are extroverts, generally happier with other people than by themselves. That being acknowledged, it is very important to recognize the necessity for your daughter to be comfortable being by herself, to get to know herself, and to increase her comfort level with being in the moment and doing nothing. Learning how to be okay with aloneness will make her feel less threatened by people who want to manipulate her by threatening to leave if she doesn't comply with their wishes—she won't fear being alone. But that's not the only reason she should develop a relationship with herself.

Having time to yourself to think is often minimized, and yet, it is incredibly important for us to recharge and renew. After a long day at work, you would probably love to have some downtime to read a book, take a walk, or just lay on your bed. Why not encourage that same downtime for your children? They are overscheduled, overtaxed, and often have no time to really figure out what they enjoy, what they may want to do, or how to just be.

During the time she gets to be alone, your daughter also has the opportunity to step back and think about and embrace all the things you are trying to teach her, and she might start to internalize these lessons into her core beliefs.

You have been teaching her a lot of important skills that will help her to feel empowered and positive about herself. In learning these skills, she will in turn know how to be compassionate and caring toward herself, which will allow her to be more so toward others, as well. To further her ability to be compassionate and caring for herself, teach her how to affirm herself. Do this by helping her validate her own feelings, thoughts, and behaviors, and tell her to praise herself for a job well done.

Also, in teaching her to speak up for herself, you are teaching her that being assertive, and caring for oneself, is not the same as being selfish or narcissistic. Being able to put your own needs first can be a healthy option, at times. The earlier your daughter learns to do this, the better.

AGE-APPROPRIATE SOLUTIONS TO THE "I'M ONLY AS GOOD AS OTHER PEOPLE THINK I AM" SYMPTOM

To help your daughter learn to value herself and not just depend on others for validation, you have to show her how to validate herself, teach her how to be alone, and help her distinguish between healthy care of herself and selfishness.

Ages 2–3

Play with your daughter. This sounds easier said than done, especially if you're a working mom with more than one child. Stop and think about how often you give her undivided (meaning, cell-phone-free) attention. Be creative about finding the time to give her this attention—cobbling ten minutes here and there (before breakfast; when she gets home from school; after you clean up from dinner). Remember, play is your daughter's primary form of exploring the world at this age. Allow her to run the playtime, which may mean fighting the urge to take over, show her how to do it, or create the story. That means allowing princess play if that's what she wants to do. But you *can* encourage healthier princess play that will help her affirm her feelings. For example, if she's pretending to be locked in the tallest tower, encourage her to figure out how she will escape (personal empowerment) rather than waiting for the prince to come and rescue her. Play provides opportunities for you to teach your daughter about the impact she has on you, how to follow rules, and how to problem-solve.

At this age, your daughter is just learning what feelings are, and how they differ from one another. Identify and label them when she expresses them and start to talk about how they are different—sad is different from mad, mad is different from happy. It is important to give her a broad foundation of emotional language.

When she expresses feelings, validate them. Remember, her feelings (anger, frustration) are valid, even if the actions she uses to express them (hitting, screaming) are not. At this age, she will act on her feelings more than she will be able to state what they are. That's to be expected, but you should continue helping her label, understand, and regulate her feelings. This age is all about learning how to talk and express themselves. It is hard to do both, even for adults. Validate how your daughter feels by identifying the feeling for her. Explain to her what is an appropriate and acceptable form of expression, and what is not. "I can tell you're very mad. But you can't hit people even if you're mad. Let's talk about being mad."

Two key components are:

1. When you talk about feelings, talk about all the ways feelings can be expressed.

2. Demonstrate what different emotions look like in your body and have your daughter do the same. For example, if she's mad, she might clench her fists or stamp her foot. This will help her know how she is feeling, and what to do about it.

Ages 4–5

Children at this age are getting a stronger sense of themselves as distinct individuals who do good and bad things. Help her learn not to equate *doing* something bad with *being* someone bad (that is, help her distinguish thought from feeling; doing from being). Reframe the idea, so she takes the onus of the situation off of herself as a person and refocuses it on her actions. Help her shift to "I did a bad thing" from "I'm bad."

Set your daughter up for success. If she demonstrates an interest or a skill in something, encourage her to pursue it. Do not push excessively or hover over her, though. Talk about how she can engage in the things she enjoys and work with her to find ways to do so. The more success you build, the more confident she will be in her own abilities.

Do not label your daughter, although you can help her label her feelings. Instead of saying, "You're so sensitive," you can say, "I can tell you're feeling sad today." Using labels limits your daughter's view of herself and the world. If one can hide behind a label, then one never has to deal with the emotions the label may stir. Try to recognize the elements behind the label, rather than using the label. You don't want your daughter to make that label her core identity.

Ages 6–8

At this age, your daughter is starting to seek more approval from her peers. She is going to be making more comparisons with regard to them and this could cause her to feel badly about the things her peers have that she does not (and vice versa). Take the time to talk about differences between people and how it is important to respect them. Help her identify her feelings and allow her to be disappointed if you say no to the things she may want.

Your daughter may also start to identify ways she is different from you as her parent. Just because she is trying to increase her sense of self and build some more independence, do not think for a minute you still do not have a significant amount of influence. You do and you must continue to model for her how to feel good in your own skin and how to handle situations as they arise. Your daughter still looks to you as a guide and will emulate what she sees.

Monitor her friends, school experience, and activities. Your daughter spends more time in school at this age than at home with you, and there are other adults in her life modeling different kinds of behaviors. Be aware of what those are and be prepared to discuss them with your daughter. As you build up your daughter's value system with her, she will be able to make decisions about whose ideas she likes and whose she does not. This continues to build over time, with your help and guidance.

It is tempting to throw your daughter into every activity in which she expresses interest, but don't overschedule her. She needs some time to herself, so provide that for her. It is important in helping her develop a true understanding of her inner self.

Building up self-worth is always a challenge, especially if you have some difficulties with it yourself. Helping your daughter understand how she feels in different situations, and how to express herself in healthy ways, will help her to build a heroine's sense of empowerment that will allow her to feel effective and confident in the world.

CHAPTER 10

Love Real People — Warts and All

PRINCESS SYMPTOM: Romance over Relationship
HEROINE VALUE: Trust in Others

UNDERSTANDING OTHERS' FLAWS

Perhaps the most significant, and damaging, consequence of Princess Syndrome is the impact it has on your daughter's ability to create authentic relationships with other people, from her early friendships to life partners. A girl who has been taught to prefer superficialities to realities is going to have a hard time coming to grips with the warts on the frog.

In our society, we're surrounded by messages that romance is all about staging performances, not about creating true intimacy. Instead of two people deciding they are ready to commit to a life together, we see reality shows with over-the-top marriage proposals complete with glass slippers and horse-drawn carriages. People eagerly wait to hear the story of how two people got engaged, to see the ring, and to discuss the details of the wedding. Somehow, we have lost the idea that what's most important is the relationship and the marriage, not the fanfare leading up to it.

Your daughter sees all of these material messages, too, and thinks that such performances form the basis for a relationship. What an unsteady foundation she will find if this is the belief she has regarding a life partner.

THE PRINCESS SYMPTOM: ROMANCE OVER RELATIONSHIP

From the time girls are small, they're deluged with messages that intimate partner relationships are about romance—the thrill of the chase, the high emotion, the drama! It is a disservice to our girls because true intimacy is about making an authentic connection with another person. Such a connection requires vulnerability, the ability to trust, and the willingness to get hurt. The development of these traits requires a level of insight that may be impossible for a person focused on appearance and style rather than substance to develop. True intimacy becomes awkward and uncomfortable for the princess.

FANTASY FRIENDS

Superficial fantasies do have their advantages. They can be a lot easier—and more fun—than real relationships! Imagining Brad Pitt whirling you off to Paris for the weekend is a lot more entertaining than dealing with the sometimes-grumpy partner you do have. A fantasy friend—that imaginary partner you sometimes daydream about—never gets mad at you, never forgets a promise, never argues with you. What's not to want or love?

If your daughter builds a picture of what her adult life will be like based on fantasy images instead of reality, she will create big problems for herself, and will end up feeling lonely and isolated. Her friends will find their Prince Charmings in healthy, balanced ways while she cannot seem to make such authentic connections.

The Addictive High of Fantasy

Living a life of fantasy is very appealing. You can pull your ideal mate out of thin air; you can create a friend who is *exactly* what you need and is always there for you. Sounds fabulous, no? Unfortunately, people who prefer to live this sort of life end up watching the reality of the world fly by. Living in fantasyland allows you to escape the pain of reality, which has ups and downs, goods and bads, and lots of things in between. Even in the best relationships, people feel occasional pain; it's a byproduct of caring about another person who is different from you and who has his (or her) own ideas, wants, and needs. We find we can protect ourselves from getting hurt (or believe we can, at least) if we focus on finding the elusive Prince Charming. By waiting for him, and believing there is only one person for us who will fit our every requirement, we may miss a lot of wonderful opportunities. Unfortunately, our culture perpetuates the belief there is such a thing as a Prince Charming, someone who will never make you feel bad, hurt your feelings, or make you feel disappointed (even by accident once in a while). If you wait long enough, of course you will find him.

The reality is we can form intimate partner relationships with any number of people. These relationships can be romantic or platonic. The tough part is putting up with the warts real people possess. So often we try to avoid these realities, and the media we are exposed to help us do this all along the way.

Fantasy Interferes with Reality

The same damaging situation exists for men who get caught up in "fantasy" appearances they are unlikely to find in reality. It is impossible for real women to compete with the airbrushed perfection of women in fashion magazines or in movies. Research has shown men who spend a lot of time focusing on celebrities (like models and movie stars) and who concentrate on appearance have difficulty connecting with real women. A man can get wrapped up in the fantasy that his partner will remain young and fit simply because models and actresses do. Yet, he is not accounting for the fact many celebrities get plastic surgery, have time to spend hours in the gym, employ chefs making them healthy foods, and engage in all sorts of other interventions in order to maintain their youthful appearance. The reality: Not every woman can look like Demi Moore when she is fifty. Most women age: their bodies sag in places, gray hair develops, muscle tone gets lost. For men caught up in their own fantasy world, the reality is difficult to handle, which then makes handling their partner's wants, needs, and expectations feel burdensome.

If a man is engaged in a mutually intimate partnership based on more than appearance, though, he can accept or even embrace her gray hair or changing body. He might see her aging as beautiful, and something that is happening to them together as they grow older while maintaining their relationship. Such imperfections can spark tenderness and compassion, and a level of understanding that cannot be obtained if one lives (or tries to live) the fantasy life.

It is easy to understand the impact of the "perfect woman" and how it can interfere with a man's ability to connect with a "real" woman. Sometimes it is more challenging to see how the fantasy images of romance make it such a challenge for women to connect with real men, but, of course, it does. Women are shown many scenarios that give her the idea "if only" she had this kind of man, life would be perfect. The question she fails to ask, similarly to men, is does that man (or woman) really exist?

RELATIONSHIP STEREOTYPES

Have you ever stopped to think about what messages are presented to you and your daughter about what kinds of relationships are out there for her? What follows are some common fantasy tropes and how they can interfere with the development of true intimacy in relationships. This is just a brief overview. If you stop and think about it yourself, you can probably identify some others.

The Strong, Silent Type

In this scenario, the seemingly inarticulate individual is actually someone who thinks and feels deeply. Despite the quiet, brooding presentation, there is a great deal of romance and caring below the surface. Truthfully, and more likely, an inarticulate he-man is probably an inarticulate he-man. He might be cute to look at, but there may be little substance beyond that.

Boy Hates Girl

This is a common movie or book plot where a man treats a woman very badly, often taking out his feelings for someone else on her, only to realize in the end (once she proves her worth) he is mistaken and she is terrific. He suddenly professes his undying love for her and they live happily ever after.

In reality, a woman often stays in these types of relationships thinking she can change him; she has the power to make him see that this is different (she is different from all the others) or he *should* be nice and caring. Women put up with this bad treatment hoping this time it will be different. Unfortunately, more often than not, a mean partner is a mean partner. Someone who treats you or your daughter badly is going to continue to do so, unless he wants to change and puts serious effort into changing. Hoping for change will not make it happen, yet so many times we do believe it will, thus buying into the fantasy.

Rescuer to the Rescue

We talked about this in-depth in Chapter 8, but it's worth repeating: Our culture abounds with messages that a woman needs to be rescued by a man—whether it's from a ferocious dog, a high-rise fire, or a life of loneliness.

The reality is a woman who needs a relationship to make her feel whole creates an impossible burden on her partner, and will most likely never be satisfied. It is so important, as we discussed before, to learn how to rely on oneself. When this happens, you are much more available to healthy relationships that come your way and much more likely to choose wisely.

Opposites Attract

It is a wonderful thought to believe you can be the yin to someone's yang. And while it's true people from different backgrounds can learn to live with and love one another, the reality is many relationships end due to fundamental incompatibilities. If your worldview is the polar opposite of your partner's, and your core values do not line up, it will be practically impossible to form and maintain intimate partner bonds. It is incredibly difficult to be vulnerable and intimate with someone when you do not agree with anything he says, believe in the things he believes in, or feel judged by him for the things you *do* believe in. Although we all can name people who contradict this idea, more often than not, it is not a situation that is going to promote the kind of relationship you would want your daughter to have.

THE DANGER OF PREFERRING FANTASY TO REALITY

Although it is so easy to get sucked into the fantasy of relationships, studies have shown people who focus on the romance of a partnership—the fantasy elements rather than the reality of hard work, compassion, and kindness—suffer significantly. A lifetime of romance does not fulfill our human need for connectedness and intimacy, and, in fact, may limit our relationships to being one-dimensional, rather than rich and full. People who routinely prefer fantasy:

- Have trouble caring for themselves and loving themselves
- Don't always know their own reality
- Mistake sex for intimacy
- Can abuse others in the name of "honesty"
- Have difficulty setting boundaries

If this sounds a little like the person described in Chapter 9, that's because the person who lets others define her self-worth is more concerned with outward appearances than with reality—just like the person who prefers fantasy romance over realistic intimacy.

Coming to Terms with Fantasy

Children don't always distinguish between reality and fantasy, and when they do, they usually prefer the fantasy. In many ways, this preference is age-appropriate, of course. It is through fantasy our children learn a lot about the world, about themselves, about relationships, and the like. However, it is when the fantasy trumps reality time and again that we have to rethink our approach. When Kate Middleton and Prince William wed, one mother reported telling her daughter about this *real* princess, only to have her daughter shrug. Says the mother, "Kate Middleton was unlike any princess she'd ever come across. Unlike Belle, Middleton had not been confined to a castle with a beast, had not languished in a tower like Rapunzel, or had not outsmarted a duo of nasty stepsisters as Cinderella did." These fantasy princesses were even more appealing than the real one!

You want your daughter to engage in pretend play and to use her imagination, and sometimes she'll want to pretend to be locked in a tall tower guarded by a dragon. But you also have to make sure your daughter learns to distinguish between fantasy and reality—and you need to ensure fantasy relationships aren't the only ones your daughter is exposed to.

Don't Sweep It under the Rug

Fantasy is big in your daughter's world, and sometimes, you cannot fight it (nor should you). Trying to use logic to explain to your daughter why fantasy doesn't fly in the real world, or using the argument, "Because it isn't reality!" is not going to get you very far. In fact, it will create more conflict and frustration for you both.

The best way to fight the unreal relationships and ideas is to model what a real and honest relationship is. It is essential for your daughter to bear witness to how adults negotiate, compromise, and occasionally put the other partner first. If you're not in a marriage, she can still see you model these behaviors in your other close relationships, such as with family and friends. She also needs to see how things go wrong, and then how they are repaired.

We often forget part of building trust between two people is based on the knowledge you can be angry, yet know the other person will not magically disappear. Showing your daughter how to argue fairly and then how to follow up and try to solve the problem, is an equally important thing, and is often rooted in the ability to communicate openly.

Model Open Communication

Open communication is the key to healthy relationships. Without it, there is no solid foundation from which to grow. Partners need to be able to speak their minds—kindly and with compassion, but directly and without fear of repercussions. Encourage this in your daughter by listening attentively to her, and showing that her opinion matters. The more you listen, the more comfortable your daughter will be in sharing, a skill that will serve her well throughout her life. This starts with the most fundamental pieces of information, and builds into the sharing of feelings and ideas. Feelings are possibly some of the most difficult things to share, and they are the primary way we can inform people what impact they have on us, and how we would like things to be.

Share Your Feelings

Emotions tell us how to act in certain situations, and they also tell other people how to react to us. By understanding other peoples' emotions, we learn how to interact with them in a variety of situations. Intimacy is achieved through sharing feelings, even negative ones. This does not mean yelling and screaming, ranting and raving, although that does happen at times, because emotions do not have logic and sometimes just take over.

Model how to express feelings appropriately by owning them and using "I" statements. Even to your young child, you can say: "I felt hurt when you did that." In this way, you are teaching your daughter it is okay to express herself openly, even if it is not something the other person may want to hear—something that happens all the time in the real world. It is important she share her feelings, though, in order to get her needs met. When things are not easy, show her the best way to handle it is to discuss the feelings and mend the relationship.

Demonstrate Forgiveness

Any relationship will experience bumps in the road. It's par for the course. For any relationship to survive, however, we have to be willing to forgive and forget. Forgiveness is not always easy, and it is an important skill to teach. This applies to forgiving yourself, too. You are going to make mistakes in your relationships, with your friends, your partner, your daughter. No one is perfect. If you get caught up in the "should'ves," you will never be able to move on and you will experience a great deal of regret.

Model forgiveness for your daughter: "I felt hurt when you did that, but I know you weren't trying to be mean. I forgive you and I love you." Find opportunities to help her model forgiveness, too. Help teach her not only to say she is sorry when necessary, but also to accept the apologies of others. She may not always want to do so, but it is an important skill for creating and maintaining healthy relationships. Of course, if she is hurt time and again by the same person, you have to help her recognize when it may be time to end a relationship. Although you can forgive, it is still important to protect yourself. The commitment made to a relationship is very important, as is the one with yourself (as we have pointed out). Teach your daughter how to identify the difference.

Show Her What Real Commitment Looks Like

Relationships require commitment; as do other activities—participation on a team, for example. Sometimes, though, if you lose interest in an activity, you can choose to stop participating. This is not as easy with relationships. In order to teach your daughter how to have commitment in her relationships, you have to show your daughter what commitment is.

Begin by following through on your promises. If you make a promise, do your best to keep it. Of course, there are times when you will have to break your promise, and when this happens, do your best to explain it to your daughter. Trust starts with you, and is an important element of commitment. If you do not follow through, how can you expect your daughter to trust you in the future? Just as she should be able to expect you to follow through, you should expect her to follow through on promises she makes. Remind her not to promise things if she does not think she will follow through, even if it seems easier to promise than to say no. Not following through creates a lot of problems in relationships she will have to repair. And what better way to stand up for herself than by being honest and direct in her interactions, although that may mean disappointing others?

Teach Her Discernment

Determining whether a relationship is overall a positive one versus a negative one is not easy because all relationships have positive and negative components. Many healthy relationships involve hurt feelings. Sometimes, though, the hurt is just the tip of the iceberg and the relationship is really unhealthy for your daughter. She may not be able to see it, and will try to fix it or accept it because she believes this is how relationships are supposed to be. If you are teaching her to be a discerning participant in relationships, she will be able to tell the difference between healthy and unhealthy ones.

Remind her to consider what she wants in a relationship, what kinds of qualities she desires in her friends, and to think about what she is willing to accept from them (since we know even friends come with warts). Although she may need you to help navigate this terrain when she is young, the more you model appropriate discernment of character, the faster she will learn to do it on her own. You can even share some experiences of your own when you have had to end friendships because you realized they were not good for you, and didn't make you feel good about yourself.

THE HEROINE VALUE: TRUST IN OTHERS

Ultimately, a person's unwillingness (or willingness, for that matter) to connect with others is about trust. If you cannot trust other people to wish you well, to love you, to care about you, to not want to hurt you, then of course it will be difficult to be as vulnerable as you need to be to create intimate relationships (whether these are with friends, life partners, or family members).

Establish Bonds

Building the foundation of trust begins with the relationship you have with your daughter. Giving your daughter a secure start in life helps her feel secure in her relationships with others throughout her life. Making sure she feels loved and wanted helps her connect to you in a way that may help her withstand peer pressure down the road. She learns how to explore the world, trusting she can always return to her home base. If you can build a positive parent-child relationship, your daughter will be well equipped to handle difficult situations throughout her life which will, unfortunately, happen.

It is not always easy to know how to create such strong bonds. It starts with leading by example. If you make your daughter, and your family, a priority, and practice what you preach, your daughter will learn what it means to be reliable and trustworthy. You must start this bond building very early on and continue it (even though she may seem to not want it) throughout her life.

Take the time to really get to know your daughter at all of her ages and stages, even the ones that are incredibly difficult and taxing. In fact, she may need you the most during these tough stages. Find the parts of her you can appreciate, and let her know what they are. Bonds are built on the trust that it is imperative you teach to your daughter. The more trust that exists, the stronger the bond can be.

Teach Trust

It cannot be said enough: Trust is the foundation for all relationships. If you do not teach your daughter what trust is and how to do it, her relationships will be like a house of cards, just waiting for the gust of wind to blow them over. Trust in her relationship with you will help her feel secure, and will thus teach her how to broaden this out to other relationships. At its most fundamental, your daughter needs to know if you say you will catch her when she jumps, you will catch her. It is important for your relationship with her that you follow through on the things you say you will do.

Honesty Is the Best Policy

We have already mentioned the importance of leading by example and listening to what your daughter expresses to you.

Trust is also built on honesty, so it is important you tell your daughter the truth. As much as you can, be honest with your daughter, in age-appropriate ways, about things she will experience. For example, if she is going to the dentist and asks if getting her cavity filled will hurt, don't lie and say no. She is looking to you for reassurance, but you have to provide it without being dishonest.

Remember, your daughter is always watching you, and will watch to see when you are being dishonest. If you ask your husband to tell your sister you are not home when she calls just because you are too tired to talk, you are actually teaching your daughter lying is okay, even if it is not a big lie. Your young daughter cannot differentiate between these kinds of lies, and she may find excuses for lying as she grows up. Lying certainly will not build trust in relationships. Teaching the importance of being honest will help to build trust in your relationship with her, and subsequently in her relationship with others. To enhance this even further, let your daughter know you appreciate when she is honest with you. The more you can build on this, the better she will be prepared for all relationships she experiences. The more trust you have, the better able she will be to see the world as it is, and find the joy and happiness within it.

AGE-APPROPRIATE SOLUTIONS FOR THE "ROMANCE OVER RELATIONSHIP" SYMPTOM

Although you do not want to take the pretend play out of your daughter's life, helping her distinguish between reality and fantasy can be helpful so she learns the importance of building positive relationships with others. It will set the stage for healthy relationships as she ages as well.

Ages 2–3

While you can, and should, encourage your daughter to participate in pretend play and imagination-building experiences, make sure she is also exposed to reality. Help her learn to do the things that are not always so fun, like waiting in line, or apologizing if she hurt her friend's feelings.

Be consistent in your message, and follow through with what you say yourself. The more consistent you are in your message about your expectations, which your daughter will learn to rely upon, the better. Starting this at an early age is crucial. Your daughter will internalize the teachings and bring them with her throughout her development.

Expose your daughter to real-life heroes, not just fantasy ones. Begin to teach her she has many options in her life, and start to show her what they are. Provide options in her pretend play to be "real" things. In addition to those princess costumes, offer doctor and police officer ones.

Ages 4–5

At this age, although she will be better able to distinguish between fantasy and reality, your daughter will still struggle with this distinction. Help her make the distinctions so she does understand what is real and what is not.

Monitor what she is watching, reading, or playing with. Be sure she is participating in things that are age-appropriate. Talk about what she is doing. Ask her questions about what she sees or reads and talk about how, although they appear real, most characters are not and the things they do cannot happen in "real" life. For example, a kiss from a prince can't really wake up a sick princess, as happens in *Sleeping Beauty* and *Snow White*, and genies, magic carpets, and caves of wonder, while a lot of fun, don't exist outside of Princess Jasmine's story.

Remind your daughter what is fantasy and what is reality. Be open to her questions when she poses them to you. Turn your conversations into an opportunity to do some research about the character she likes, or to learn more about the story she is enamored with.

Find out what she likes about the fantasy characters she focuses on. Help her to explain what characteristics they have that she may want. Maybe some of them are realistic goals.

Ages 6–8

Your daughter can more readily distinguish between fantasy and reality now, but she's still getting messages she may think are true and real because they're so pervasive. They just are presented to her in a different way. Rather than being in cartoons and fantasy stories, advertisers present a great deal of fantastical ideas to her she has to learn how to weed through. Help her to understand the meaning behind the advertisements, and that just because the picture makes it seem like life will be better with that special outfit, it is not necessarily true.

Continue to teach her the importance of building trust in relationships and help her understand that getting to know people takes time, patience, and compassion.

Talk with her about the qualities she would like in her friends, and help provide her with opportunities to find people with those traits.

Teaching your daughter how to build positive and healthy relationships in her life is so important, and, as with most things, it starts with you. You are the first relationship she enters into, and through this relationship, she will learn how to have others.

If you raise her to be a princess, relying on others, expecting others to cater to her every whim, she will not be able to have relationships that are meaningful. If you work to instill the heroine values in her, she will be open and honest, and available to any prince (or frog) that comes her way.

CONCLUSION

Living Happily Ever After

While it may seem as though you have to slay an enormous dragon (which is composed of peers, media, and culture) in order to save your daughter from the perils of Princess Syndrome, remember you have a very distinctive advantage: you are her parent. You are the single greatest influence in her life beginning in her formative years and onward.

Although it may seem overwhelming to combat all of the messages she receives, it is possible, and you *can* make a difference in your daughter's life. It will take work, effort, and involvement, of course, but it's worth every bit of commitment to watch your daughter develop into the strong heroine you know she can be. By implementing some of these changes now, you will help your daughter learn to be empowered, determined, and committed to making the life *she* wants. She will see the limitations that could be in her way if she remained a princess and she'll choose to be a heroine instead. What could make you more proud than that?

Though a younger girl is less able to understand some of the concepts we talked about, take heart: You have much more influence over these types of behaviors when she is two or three. You are her primary teacher, and it is important you start setting the stage early for how you want to see her later. She may be a heroine-in-training at age two, and because of the things you are teaching her, and the expectations and values you impart, she will be able to be a full heroine by age eight. Although her confidence may be challenged at different times, especially as she is a preteen and teenager, if she has these values as her core beliefs, she will have a place to go back to in order to refuel and continue to feel confident and self-assured.

Instead of thinking of your task as insurmountable, shift your thinking so you handle one "symptom" at a time. As you may have noticed, many of the princess symptoms build on one another. If you can change one, it may start a ripple effect in helping you correct the others. As you correct one princess symptom, you'll go a long way toward building the heroine values. If you promote the idea of independence and commitment, while continuing to teach her how to use her mind and think for herself and you start this early, you are teaching her the heroine values you really prize and others prize as well. Taking these steps now will set the stage for later in her life, especially when the pressures are even greater.

By committing to the Princess Recovery Program, you can help put your daughter on the road to creating her own, real happily ever after.

Children's Books for Heroines

AGES 2–3

Alice the Fairy by David Shannon
I Know a Rhino by Charles Fuge
It's a Jungle in Here by Deanne Lee Bingham
Just Like Daddy by Frank Asch
The Mixed-Up Chameleon by Eric Carle
The Mommy Book by Todd Parr
The Paper Bag Princess by Robert N. Munsch
Slide, Already! by Kit Allen
Winners Never Quit by Mia Hamm

AGES 4–5

Big Bouffant by Kate Hosford
Lucy and the Bully by Claire Alexander
My Name Is Not Isabella by Jennifer Fosberry
Not All Princesses Dress in Pink by Jane Yolen and Heidi E.Y. Stemple
Princess Backwards by Jane Gray
Princess Smartypants by Babette Cole
Violet the Pilot by Steve Breen
You Can't Do That, Amelia by Kimberly Wagner Klier
What Will I Be? by Dawne Allette

AGES 6–8

Amazons! Women Warriors of the World by Sally Pomme Clayton

The Daring Book for Girls by Andrea J. Buchanan and Miriam Peskowitz

Earth to Audrey by Susan Hughes

Little House on the Prairie series by Laura Ingalls Wilder

Madam President by Lane Smith

The Princess Knight by Cornelia Funke

Seven Brave Women by Betsy Gould Hearne

Watch Out for Clever Women! by Joe Hayes

Healthy Princess Play Ideas

If you want to help your daughter shed the princess stereotypes (or avoid them altogether) but you're just not sure how to go about it, consider encouraging the following play ideas. Instead of trying to convince your three-year-old that it's no fun to pretend to be princesses, turn some of the traditional games on their heads.

BUILD A CASTLE

When your daughter wants to be rescued from the castle, tell her you'd rather *build* a castle. Get out the blocks and build a miniature medieval palace. Or, drape a blanket over two chairs and call it a tower instead of a fort. Have your daughter sketch a castle, or draw a floor plan of one together. For an older child, you can research different types of castles, what types of rooms and buildings they include, and what they look like.

DESIGN A DRESS

Instead of just playing dress up in a princess gown, your daughter (with your help) can create her own look. Have her add a scarf to your old dress, or a cape to her T-shirt and shorts. Or, design a dress on paper. Sketch what it would look like and color it in with crayons or markers. You could also use fabric swatches and leftover trim to create a dress for a paper doll. Talk about fabric, color, style—describe what you like and why and encourage your daughter to do the same.

PLAY THE OTHER ROLES

If your daughter wants to pretend to be princesses, propose that you try out other roles she may be familiar with from the stories and movies. What about playing the Beast, or Doc, or even the Evil Queen? Imagine what those characters' lives must be like. Act out before and after scenes, too. What was the Beast like before he was turned into the Beast—and after he was turned back into a man? What was Doc like before Snow White came to the cottage? What was he like after she left with her prince? This could be an opportunity to invent all kinds of outcomes. Was Doc sad to see Snow White go? Or glad that he could stop washing up before dinner?

MAKE A REAL TEA PARTY

Instead of pretending to serve tea to her princess dolls, why not have a real tea party? Make some real recipes, such as tea sandwiches or tiny cakes, and serve them to each other with lemonade or sweet tea. Invite other members of the family to partake, or have her friends over and let them all participate in measuring, mixing, chopping, serving, and cleaning up afterward.

TEACH HER HOW TO DANCE AT THE BALL

If your daughter delights in the idea of going to the ball, find an aspect that is worth encouraging, such as learning to dance. Teach her some simple steps, turn on the music, and show your stuff! Or, let her pick the music and show *you* some dance steps.

LEARN ABOUT REAL PRINCESSES

When your daughter waxes romantic about what it would be like to be a princess, give her a reality check—one that is still interesting and entertaining—by helping her find out what it's like to be a real princess. Show her pictures of real-life princesses like Catherine Middleton and talk about what her life is like. What kinds of duties and obligations must she fulfill? How is her life different from other women her age? Read age-appropriate biographies of other princesses, such as Princess Di.

PLAY A PIRATE-PRINCESS

Add another dimension to princess role-playing by adding another noun to princess: pirate, doctor, explorer, astronaut. Explore with your daughter how this additional role would change some aspects of being a princess. Maybe she would have to trade her tiara for a stethoscope. Maybe she would wield a sword instead of a magic wand. Encourage her to use her imagination to create all kinds of hyphenated princesses.

SAVE THE DRAGON

Instead of playing the princess waiting to be rescued, encourage your daughter to be the rescuer. Explain the plight of a poor, wandering dragon who has been trapped in an enchanted forest. What will your daughter have to do to free it?

Index